MINDFUL NEGOTIATION

"A wealth of great advice on how to harness the power of mindfulness to create maximum value for everyone. Inspiring, engaging and provides useful tools that can be applied immediately. A must read for all negotiators wanting to create more valuable agreements".

— **Meg McKenna**, Vice President, Americas, Advanced Surgery, Baxter Healthcare Corporation

"The self-awareness on how to master emotions during the negotiation through mindfulness practice, is a significant enhancement that I have not seen in commercial negotiations training or literature before, and it is critical to success. This book guides you from theory to practice"

— **Andy Molnar**, Medical Devices President & CEO

"Gaëtan is masterful in introducing the powerful role that mindfulness can play in the negotiation process. His direct and engaging writing style, his real-life examples and his provocative questions will keep you engaged from start to finish. The fact that negotiating is such a natural part of our daily life makes this book a must read, especially when combined with such a clear understanding of what we can do to keep our egos in check at every step of the negotiation process."

— **Charles Brassard**, President of Impact Coaching Inc.

"Finally, a long overdue fresh perspective on what drives successful negotiations! In this era of automation and AI applications, Gaëtan goes beyond the methodology that most books focus on and brings to light how egos and emotions are the true drivers of success or failure. A must read for whoever is interested in win-win deals!"

— **François Drolet**, Director, Public Affairs, Access, Health Policy & Stakeholder Engagement Roche Diagnostics

"As a seasoned corporate executive, I picked up this book thinking I would be inspired by or reminded of a couple of good tips and tricks for applying in business and negotiations specifically. I did get that for sure, but what I didn't expect was to come away feeling like I have a new set of tools for not only applying immediately to negotiations, but also more deeply for my own personal growth, and relationships as well. Mindfulness has taken on a whole new and enhanced meaning to me and I know I will be referencing *Mindful NEGOtiation's* content as I continue to exercise my new and more mindful muscle in the months to come."

— **Clare Dunis**, Marketing & Sales Executive

"You know a book is good when it sticks with you. That is what this book did for me. Being a negotiator by trade, I have an interest in the topic but most books I read about negotiations leave me underwhelmed. That was not the case with this book, it isn't your typical negotiation book. It digs deep into the heart of what is really going on in a negotiation; all the unspoken things. It then takes those unspoken truths and provides the tools to help you effectively analyze the situation and deliver a valuable outcome for everyone. I plan to put the learnings from this book to use both professionally and personally. *Mindful NEGOtiation* is a great read if you are ready to take a hard look in the mirror."

— **Millie Davis**, Negotiation Consultant

"Planning & having a framework are key, being in control of our ego is masterful. This what this book is offering: an opportunity to bring mindfulness to the negotiation table allowing us to execute under stress."

—Vice President, Health Policy and Patient Access

MINDFUL
NEGOTIATION

Becoming More Aware in the Moment, Conquering Your Ego
and Getting Everyone What They Really Want

GAËTAN PELLERIN

NEW YORK

LONDON • NASHVILLE • MELBOURNE • VANCOUVER

MINDFUL NEGOTIATION

Becoming More Aware in the Moment, Conquering Your Ego
and Getting Everyone What They Really Want

© 2021 **GAËTAN PELLERIN**

Published in New York, New York, by Morgan James Publishing. Morgan James is a
trademark of Morgan James, LLC. www.MorganJamesPublishing.com

ISBN 978-1-63195-442-9 paperback
ISBN 978-1-63195-443-6 eBook
Library of Congress Control Number: 2020923517

Cover Design by:
Andrea Schmidt,
a-schmidt.com

Morgan James is a proud partner of Habitat for Humanity Peninsula
and Greater Williamsburg. Partners in building since 2006.

Get involved today! Visit
www.MorganJamesBuilds.com

Pamela Pritchard, this book is dedicated to you. I know you are here in this moment from high above. You were my executive coach and my friend. You brought me to the Diamond approach for my spiritual development. "You are ripe for it," you said. You were right. You believed in me and never judged me. Your kindness and compassion allowed me to trust you in my ability to grow. I felt your presence with me along the way of writing this book. Love you forever.

TABLE OF CONTENTS

ACKNOWLEDGEMENTS

This book would not have existed as the way it is now without the coaching, editing, advice, and recommendations from my book coach and editor James Ranson, aka The Master Wordsmith™. Thank you, James, for understanding my voice, for your patience and encouragement, and for all the ways you creatively supported this book.

Andrea Schmidt, I want to thank you for the fantastic book cover design matching exactly what I was envisioning. David Hancock, CEO of Morgan James Publishing, thank you for taking the time to read my manuscript and connect with me in such a way that built trust from the first call. Thank you for agreeing to publish this book. Jim Howard, Margo Toulouse, Nickcole Watkins and all others at Morgan James Publishing, your passion, ability to support makes a big difference. Thank you for bringing my book to life.

This book has been a life project for five years, and many people in my life influenced and inspired me to write this book:

Thomas Weinberg, Diamond Approach teacher: thank you for your teaching, kindness and compassion toward my spiritual development. Lauren Taylor, also Diamond Approach teacher, thank you for your on-going guidance and compassion along the road to writing this book. To all my fellow diamond seekers, thank you for your presence, your acceptance, and support.

I want to thank Patti Channer for renting her house in Ventura, CA, for three months, to support my dream of living in California. Thank you for treating me as a family member. Kathleen Morris, you are my spiritual mother. Thank you for your kindness, active listening, and moral support. I love you both.

A special thanks to Charles Brassard, my coaching teacher, and friend. You are an amazing individual, and you had a front-row seat to my on-going development. Thank you for your on-going support, encouraging me, and reviewing twice my manuscript and providing such valuable feedback.

Elizabeth Gilbert, thank you for writing: BIG MAGIC: creative living beyond fear. Your book really helped me to keep moving forward and not let my fears control my creativity.

Ross Lagumina, thank you for giving me a copy of HEED YOUR CALL by David M. Howitt. It was a great gift that inspired me to move forward with my book.

A special thanks to Seth Bartlett, François Drolet, Clare Dunis, Ella G Irwin, Meg McKenna Andy Molnar, Millie and Simon (you know who you are) for taking the time to read and in some cases, re-read my manuscript and provide such valuable feedback.

A special thanks to Brian Buck: I genuinely enjoy our conversations about ego and life. Thank you for your on-going support and for taking the time to read twice my manuscript and provide invaluable tips and pieces of advice.

I can't stop here without talking about my family: Mom and Dad, thank you so much for your love and support. You always believed in me. It means the world to me. Kevin, my son & Justine, Daniel, my brother & Mireille, thank you for your on-going love, support, and encouragement.

Chris, my beautiful wife, I'm so grateful that you are in my life. Thank you for your unconditional love and on-going support. I love you so much.

PART ONE

THE FOUNDATION

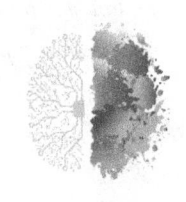

MEET ALEXIS

The meeting was not going well.

"You did what?!" Jorge shouted.

"I...may have lost the Healthcare Mountain Group account," Alexis repeated, trying (and failing) to hold eye contact with her boss.

Jorge's fists clenched. "That's not possible. I told you everything you needed to say to them. I told you exactly what we can and can't give them. And I told you exactly how to beat that jerk, Lucas, they always send to negotiate with us. And now you're telling me you've lost the account—your biggest account, the one I gave you to as your first assignment in the leadership development program I nominated you for?"

Alexis swallowed and gave a small nod, staring at the edge of Jorge's desk.

Jorge threw up his hands and dropped into his chair. "Okay, start at the beginning. Tell me exactly what happened."

"Well, I started out like you said, telling Lucas he couldn't keep paying the discounted prices from the last contract anymore. Then I said the contract was four months late for renewal and that the one-month extensions they'd been getting since then won't work anymore. And then I said their contract would expire at the end of this month, so unless they agree with our proposal, everything will go to list price."

"Okay, that sounds like everything I told you to say," said Jorge. "What happened next?"

"Lucas asked me what the list price was, which surprised me because I'm sure he knew it, and so I told him, and then I told him again that they'd been getting a huge

discount for four months and that they needed to either sign the contract or pay the list price."

"Mmhmm, and then?"

"Well…then Lucas kind of flipped out. He told me the deal was crap, that there was no way they would renew the contract at our proposed price, and that I'd better go back here and sharpen my pencil if I wanted him to renew the contract at all instead of going somewhere else! He was so angry I couldn't think of anything to say. I couldn't even move!"

"Oh. And so you…what? Just sat there and took that from him? Unbelievable." Jorge threw up his hands again.

"What else could I do?" Alexis wailed. "It's not like I've had any negotiation training, not like you and the others in this leadership development program! I had no idea what I was doing. I was just repeating what you told me to say!"

"And that should be enough! Everyone else I've mentored in this leadership development program has done just fine in situations like the one you just blew. And you have had negotiation training—we covered it during your onboarding when you joined the company. You had everything you needed, and you blew it."

Alexis sighed and dropped her eyes to the desktop again. "Maybe I could have done better," she ventured.

"Darn right you could have. But you might get another chance. You said Lucas sent you back here to come up with a different proposal for the contract?"

"I think so," said Alexis. "I'm pretty sure that's what he meant by going back and sharpening my pencil. And he didn't say he was going to go to our competitors just yet. I think I've got one more chance."

"Okay," said Jorge. "Here's what we're going to do. I want you to schedule another call with that moron for the week after next. Then you'll offer him five percent off the proposed price in return for a three-year contract rather than two. And this time, you will make that stick, do you understand?"

"But what if he—"

"Yes or no, Alexis? You've got to deliver if you're going to stay in this leadership program, and that means you've got to learn to be aggressive. Can you do it?"

Alexis nodded miserably. "Yes, sir."

A few minutes later, Alexis left Jorge's office and walked back across the medical sales floor, looking at her shoes.

"Mexican for lunch today?" she heard as she passed Kamal's desk.

"Sure, whatever," she mumbled, dropping her purse and briefcase on her desk.

"Whoa, sister, hold on a sec!" Kamal said. "That didn't sound like my favorite cheerful Alexis. You know, the one who's addicted to fajitas? The one who always tries to get us to do Mexican for lunch? The one who hides guacamole in her top left drawer?"

"Hush, you," Alexis grumbled. "I should never have told you about my guac stash." She looked up at her friend and co-worker of two and a half years. "Mexican is fine. In fact, it's more than fine—I need it after the meeting I just had."

"Oh, sweetie, I hear that. I think most of the office heard it. Jorge is a tough cookie, for sure."

"That's…one way to put it," said Alexis. "It's also the second time I've been yelled at today, and it's not even lunchtime! And I only did what I was told to do in the first place—how is this my fault?" She sighed and put her head down on the desk.

"Negotiation isn't easy. But it's not as hard as all that, either" said Kamal. "What are you struggling with?"

"You mean aside from everything?" Alexis huffed. "It's easy for you to say it's not that hard—you've been here for years and have had training and actually know what you're doing. Same with Jonathan and Ling and Leilani and Peter and everyone in our lunch group. I mean, don't get me wrong, I love that you all have sort of adopted me, but I feel so far behind where you guys are. How am I ever supposed to get there, let alone be this aggressive dynamo Jorge wants me to be? I thought I was going to get bounced out of the leadership development program just now, if not outright fired! Don't you get it, Kamal? I have no idea what I'm doing, and Jorge's so-called mentoring is making things worse, not better!"

Kamal gave Alexis a gentle smile. "Did that help? Or do you need the guac stash, too?"

Alexis managed a weak chuckle. "I always need the guac stash, and you know it. But seriously, I really do feel lost here. How do you and Jonathan and the rest do it? You're like the best sales reps in the company, and I don't ever hear about you being super aggressive when you negotiate! You never even get mad—not even when I rant at you like I just did. What's your secret? Please tell me!"

Kamal was quiet for a moment. Then he stood up and said, "Let's take an early lunch today." Alexis, bewildered, followed her co-worker out of the office building and down the block to Chico's Taqueria. Kamal said nothing as they walked, sending several text messages on his phone.

As they found a table at the restaurant, Jonathan joined them. "I got your text on my way back in from my meeting, Kamal," he said, dropping his coat in an empty chair. "Alexis, you doing okay?"

"I've been better. I'm sure Kamal mentioned my epic rant in his message," Alexis said, arching an eyebrow at Kamal.

"You? Rant? Never," Kamal stated, winking at her. Alexis stuck her tongue out at him.

"Look, Alexis," said Jonathan. "Kamal did tell me you had a disaster of a negotiation this morning, and that Jorge let you have it afterward. He also said you want some help with the whole negotiation thing so that you can get Jorge off your back. Does that sound about right?"

Alexis nodded, then shook her head, then nodded again. Kamal and Jonathan traded looks. "Well, that certainly clears it up," Kamal laughed.

"No, what I mean is that yes, I want to get better at negotiating, but no, I don't want to have to do it the way Jorge wants me to. He keeps telling me to be more aggressive and beat the other side, but when I try to do that, it blows up in my face and I just freeze. I literally couldn't move when Lucas was yelling at me this morning and dealing with Jorge wasn't much better."

"Ah," said Jonathan, leaning forward. "That's what I was hoping to hear."

Alexis blinked. "What? That was one of the worst mornings of my life!"

Jonathan laughed gently. "No, not that. I meant that you don't want to do everything Jorge's way. That's what I was hoping you'd say. I was planning on asking you that question myself in a sec, but you beat me to it."

"But why does that matter so much?" Alexis was getting more confused by the second.

"It matters," said Kamal, "for the same reason it matters that we're having this chat at Chico's rather than at our desks."

"Okay, now I'm really lost," said Alexis. "So, while I sit here and drown my morning in these delicious free tortilla chips, I need you two to drop the cryptic stuff and tell me what's going on here. Please?"

"Alright, I'm sorry," said Jonathan. "The reason we're talking here, and the reason I wanted to know if you were attached to Jorge's approach, is because I know someone who could help you get better at negotiation. But there are two catches: she doesn't work for our company, and her approach is pretty much the opposite of Jorge's."

"So, before Jonathan introduces her to anyone from our office," continued Kamal, "He needs to make sure that a different approach is okay—and that the person is okay with basically going behind the company's back."

"I see," said Alexis. "It's not illegal to work with an outside coach or anything, is it?"

"No, of course not," said Jonathan. "But I don't imagine Jorge would like it much, do you?"

"No, he'd hate it," agreed Alexis. "If I were to do something like this, I couldn't tell him."

"Well, you could…but I'd suggest not doing it right away," said Kamal. "I've seen a few people like Jorge come and go from this company, and they care about results more than anything else. If you start making deals, he won't care how you do it. It's only when you don't make them that he'll give you a hard time about doing everything his way."

"So…I'd start working with this negotiation coach on my own time, but not tell Jorge about it until I start getting better results?"

"Something like that. Use your best judgment," said Kamal.

"Alright, let's say I'm interested," said Alexis. "Who is this coach, and how can I be sure she's the best person to help me?"

"First of all, she's my Aunt Mia," said Jonathan, "so I've literally known her all my life. More importantly, she's also been an executive coach specializing in negotiation for over a decade. She has her own company doing it, in fact. Works with C-suite execs all over the world. But she also has a thing for helping newbies learn the ropes. Someone taught her how to negotiate without being a total jerk when she was right where you are now, and she likes to pay it forward."

A lightbulb went on in Alexis's mind. "That's your secret, isn't it, Kamal? You've worked with her before, haven't you?"

Kamal grinned a very wide grin. "You bet I have, sweetie. So has Jon here, obviously, and so has most of the rest of our little lunch group."

"There's a reason we do so well at negotiating contracts, Alexis," said Jonathan, "and it has nothing to do with people like Jorge. Mia taught us all to negotiate from the inside out, to start with the last thing the Jorges of the world tend to think about."

"What's that?" asked Alexis.

"Well, Mia does a better job of explaining it than I will, but let's just say it starts with those emotions that paralyzed you this morning and goes from there. So, what do you think? Should I set up a lunch meeting with you and Aunt Mia?"

Alexis nodded firmly. "Yes, please. I've got two weeks to get ready to save the HMG account, and I need all the help I can get."

"Sounds like a plan," said Jonathan. "I'll set it up."

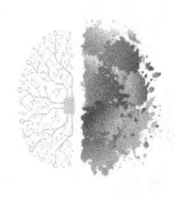

INTRODUCTION

Negotiation is a lot like mountain climbing.

Climbing a mountain may sound easy if you've never done it before—you just keep going up until there's no more up to go to, right? Even as you do some training and start to know what to expect, you still probably feel like "I've got this! It might be a bit of a challenge, but I know what to do, and I'll come out on top, no problem."

But then as you start to actually climb the mountain, you realize no amount of reading books or training on a climbing wall can prepare you for what you're facing. The trail is steep. Your pack is heavy. Breathing is getting harder. It's cold, even though the sun's still out…and those clouds on the horizon are looking pretty dark. You've been walking for hours and…wait…where are you again? Where did the trail go? And now it's starting to snow! Who knows how to build a fire in the snow? The wind is so sharp you can't feel your hands or face anymore. We brought a tent, right? Was that a bear on the other side of those trees? Help!

Like mountain climbing, negotiation looks easy from the outside…until you have to do it yourself. Then, as suddenly as a snowstorm or an avalanche blowing down the mountainside, you feel completely unprepared, out of control, and doomed. Your stress level goes through the roof, everything starts moving way too fast, you don't understand any of what's happening, and all you want to do is get out of there as quickly as possible!

Why does this happen? How can someone as smart, talented, skilled, and trained as you go from confident and competent to uncontrolled and totally freaked out in only a few moments of a negotiation meeting? Especially when there's no snowstorm or avalanche to be afraid of—you're in no physical danger at all!

What's really happening here is that you're dealing with something none of your intellect, talent, skill, or training has prepared you for: emotions.

You're *afraid* you might lose the deal. You're *intimidated* by the other person. You're *insecure* about your own sense of incompetence. You feel *judged* by your boss. You're *ashamed* that you don't already know how to negotiate well. You're *scared* that your job could depend on what happens in the next ten minutes. You're *jealous* of your co-workers—how are they so good at this? You're *angry* at yourself—why do I suck at this? Maybe you want to lash out at the people across the table—or maybe you want to run away, freeze, or even back down entirely.

None of these emotions are new. You've felt them before. But most of the time, as you go about your work, you don't have to face them. You can focus on your intellect, your talent, your skills, and your training, and that's enough.

But negotiation is different. When you negotiate, all of your emotions come out of hiding at once.

This is why negotiation is so complicated and stressful—and why most people dread doing it. Even if you know a lot of negotiation strategies and tactics, I bet you still struggle when you get emotional—or when the other side does. Very few people, even experienced experts, are capable of negotiating well in real time and under stress through skills and techniques alone. You absolutely can master negotiation skills and still fail at negotiating.

Why? Because to succeed in business and to negotiate well, you are told to rationalize everything, to numb your emotions and feel nothing. The theory behind that is when you cut yourself off from emotions, work becomes easier to navigate, strategies are quicker to plan, and deals are more comfortable to negotiate. When you don't have to take the time to deal with everyone's emotions—and the varying reactions everyone has to them—you can make everything black and white and close the deal more efficiently.

The majority of negotiation trainings, therefore, focus on the structure and methodology of the negotiation—the what, how, and when of closing the deal. And there's nothing wrong with that—in fact, understanding and implementing structure and methodology are essential to a successful negotiation.

They just aren't *all* you need.

See, structures and methodologies are rational—but human beings are emotional. Even if we're not supposed to be—sometimes, especially because we're not supposed to be! That situation where you don't have to take the time to deal with emotions, as ideal as it sounds, doesn't really exist.

The likelihood that you'll deal with emotion during negotiation is almost 100%. And even if you manage to stay utterly rational for a while, the *other* person will almost certainly display emotions of their own, which will probably trigger yours.

All of a sudden, the logical structure can't support the negotiation anymore. Emotions are now in control on both sides—which means the negotiation is now *out* of control.

The truth is negotiation has nothing to do with being rational. It's all about emotions. Successful negotiation doesn't just require intellect, talent, skill, and training…it also requires the ability to handle emotions in real time.

This is why negotiation fails for so many, so often. Way too many people negotiate poorly because they fall victim to their own emotions and don't know how to. Worst of all, these people—people like you and me—may not even be aware of the problem. It's all too easy to think, "I'm just bad at negotiating, no wonder I failed" or "I'm great at negotiating—I just had an off day" when in reality, you're missing a key piece of the puzzle.

So, what's the solution?

The solution is to handle your emotions before they get a chance to take over. And the only way to avoid being controlled by your emotions during the negotiation process is to be present and mindful during the entire negotiation.

Being mindful will help you be aware of your feelings, and the other person's emotions as well, so you can avoid becoming their victim.

Imagine being fully aware of each feeling as it arises, recognizing that it's not in control of you or of the situation, and becoming an *observer* of that emotion instead of a *victim* of it. Imagine walking into a meeting where you know you have to turn down an offer, not with a sense of panic, stress, and shame… but with the calm assurance that even though things aren't great, you can still have a positive, healthy interchange and find a deal both sides can work with. How much better would that feel? How much more comfortable would you be negotiating in the future? How much more likely is it that those negotiations would go well for you?

If you are present to what is going on internally, you can change the outcome of negotiation for good.

Really. Mindfulness has that power! By defeating the feeling that emotion has total control of the meeting (on both sides!), your mindfulness allows both you and the people across the table to handle their emotions, stop feeling like powerless victims, and find or create solutions that may not have been acceptable (or even on the radar) before. And best of all, that can happen whether or not the other side is being mindful at all. If *you* are mindful, you can turn the negotiation into calm collaboration, no matter what's happening opposite you.

If you are mindful of your emotions, you can be a good negotiator, even if you don't master all negotiation skills. However, you can't be a great negotiator if you rely strictly on skills without understanding how mindfulness can help you be in control of your emotions.

How do I know this?

I've been a professional negotiator for close to three decades—as a sales expert, negotiation skills trainer, and negotiation strategy consultant for Fortune 500 companies around the globe. But I've also always been intrigued by the nature of people and different cultures. I love coaching and consulting to help people be more in control of their lives. I'm a certified integral executive coach, and I've been actively involved in my own personal growth since 2010.

My growth work has focused on being mindful, and on how the blending of mindfulness with expertise can make the skills even stronger. It's helped me be more aware of emotions and understand their impact on my life and my clients' lives. It's shown me how often our emotions control us, most of the time, without us even being aware of it. And it's given me a new perspective on the world of negotiation: most coaches, authors, and trainers in the field refrain from discussing how emotionally attached we truly are when we step into a negotiation.

So, I'm writing this book from the perspective that all of us are emotional human beings that, by default, listen to and fall victim to our own emotions when we try to negotiate. In the following pages, I offer you the ability to get better at negotiation through mindfulness, as well as the chance to learn negotiation skills you can use even when you're dealing with emotion.

Fair warning, this book will challenge you. Emotions are uncomfortable to face—that's why we don't want to face them (and why we dread negotiation so much!). There will be some moments in the text that will take you out of your comfort zone, bring you face to face with parts of yourself you may not want to see, and push you to think about long-held beliefs and ideas in new ways. I encourage you to embrace these moments and learn everything they can teach you.

Similarly, my writing style is like my coaching style—challenging and compassionate. I will challenge your perception of negotiation and cut through the BS around what you think you already know, while also holding space for you to experiment and learn without fear of failure. I ask you to read this book with an open mind, just as you would approach an in-person coaching session.

Also, this is an experiential book. The best way to get value from it is to consider this reading as an experience where you don't just read, you practice. My goal is that by the end of the book, you not only understand the concepts and ideas I've shared, but you've already started using them to become a better negotiator.

This book has two different parts.

Part One, chapters 1 through 5, will introduce and explore the concept of ego, emotions, mindfulness, and the methodology for mindful change. Some of the chapters in Part One will conclude with exercises to further understand and implement the material.

Part Two, chapters 6 through 11, will cover the entire negotiation process, starting with preparation and finishing with closing the deal. We will use the process to explore the negotiation situations where your emotions could be triggered, and the negative impacts those moments can have on the negotiation itself. I will guide you through an innovative experiential model and approach that will help you be aware of what is going on in the moment and how you can change your behavior to put you and not your emotions in control of the situation.

Within and around these two parts is a story that demonstrates and illustrates the teachings of both. In it, you'll follow a young medical sales consultant, Alexis, through a tough contract negotiation, as she learns and begins to apply principles of mindfulness.

Because Part Two follows the major steps in a negotiation process, and because its teaching relies on the concepts explained in Part One, I strongly recommend you read the book in order from start to finish rather than skipping around. This strategy will also let you follow along with Alexis as she learns the same lessons! If you are more interested in specific chapters or if you have an urgent need to jump to a particular section, that's okay, but I still recommend reading Part One first, so you'll have the book's framework in mind.

Like climbing a mountain, negotiation is a challenge. But when you embrace that challenge mindfully, you'll find your way to the top with ease, purpose, and triumph. So, if you're ready to learn the missing piece to negotiation success, read on!

PART 1

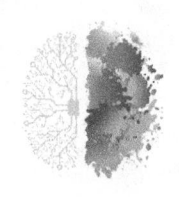

ALEXIS HAS LUNCH
WITH COACH MIA

"...and so now I just feel like I suck. At my job, at negotiation, at being the person my boss and mentor wants me to be, at everything," Alexis finished in a rush, then drained her glass of water in one gulp.

It was three days later, and Alexis had taken her lunch break a bit early again, this time to meet Jonathan's aunt, Mia, at a café across town. Mia was a sharply dressed woman in her forties, with a firm handshake and a kind smile for the anxious Alexis. Alexis was usually more reserved at first, but something about Mia's nature made her pour her heart about the Lucas/Jorge situation. Mia sat quietly while Alexis talked herself out, occasionally making a note on a small notepad.

"It sounds like you feel you should be better at this than you think you are," observed Mia. "Is that a fair statement?"

"God, yes," said Alexis. "That's exactly it! I'm in the fast track leadership development program. I'm being mentored by a manager who selected me personally, and I've apparently had the same negotiation training everyone else in the company had...why can't I get this right?"

"Do you think you could be working harder?"

Alexis frowned. "No, I don't think that's it. I already work hard—that's what got Jorge to notice me for the leadership program in the first place. This isn't me being lazy or wanting someone else to solve my problems for me! It's me feeling really over my head and out of character with what I'm being asked to do."

Mia made another note. "What do you think the consequences will be if you don't solve this?"

"Well, I'll probably lose the fast track leadership opportunity at the very least, which will hurt my future with the company and any recommendations I'd get from them down the line. I don't think I'm at risk for getting fired just yet, but I'd certainly be higher on the list for any layoffs that might come up later."

"And how do you feel about that possibility?"

"Scared," Alexis said flatly. "Really scared. And, um…a little ashamed. Like I'd have let myself down."

"Can you tell me how you were feeling throughout the meeting?"

"Um…anxious? Unsure? And scared, yeah, definitely scared, too."

"Can you tell me when exactly you felt those things?"

Alexis screwed up her forehead in thought. "Well…I'm not sure. I feel like I was anxious and unsure the whole time, really. And I got scared when Lucas started yelling at me, I guess that's a specific moment. Why does when I felt what matter?"

Mia seemed to ignore the question. "And can you tell me why you felt anxious, unsure, and scared?"

"I don't know…I was anxious because this contract is a big deal, I guess. And unsure because I've never negotiated anything this big. And scared because I was getting yelled at. Why do my feelings—"

Mia cut her off. "Do you think you could have done anything differently?"

Alexis found herself gripping her soup spoon so tightly her fingers had turned white. "No! Haven't you heard anything I said? If I could have done anything differently, I would have! I couldn't even move or think of anything to say once Lucas started shouting at me! Look, if you're not going to help me, just tell me now so I can get back to work and try to salvage this myself!"

Alexis stopped abruptly, realizing several other café patrons were now staring at her. "Sorry," she mumbled, staring into her half-eaten bowl of tomato soup. "I guess I'll go now. I'm sure you don't need to work with someone this emotional. Really, I—" She broke off when a warm hand closed on hers.

"It's totally fine, Alexis. I get it. Feeling emotions like that when you relive this kind of experience is completely understandable. Believe me when I say you have nothing to feel ashamed about," said Mia.

Alexis made herself look up. "Are you sure?"

Mia smiled at her. "Completely sure. And I want to thank you for starting by sharing so much about yourself with a complete stranger. I'm sure it felt a little strange, but I promise there's a reason I wanted to get to know you and your situation before we started discussing how I might help you."

"Of course, it's fine," said Alexis, feeling not quite as confident as she wanted to sound.

"Now, the first thing I want to tell you, Alexis, is that you're not alone in facing a situation like this, or in feeling scared and ashamed about it," said Mia, smiling reassuringly at the younger woman.

"I'm not?" Alexis began, then caught herself. "I mean, of course I'm not. There are hundreds of people—thousands—who negotiate every day. I'm sure some of them suck at it, too. I just, um…don't seem to know any of them."

Mia's smile grew broader. "You'd be surprised. For one thing, many more people struggle with negotiation than will ever admit it. For another, most people who think they're good at negotiation actually aren't—or at least nowhere near as good as they believe they are. And for a third, having negotiation training, especially the kind they teach the biology majors like you that they recruit for medical sales, doesn't automatically mean you'll know everything there is to know about negotiation—or that you should."

Alexis felt a wave of relief. "So, I'm not actually a ginormous failure?"

Mia laughed out loud, a hearty laugh that Alexis couldn't help joining in. "Oh no, Alexis, far from it! What you are is a very sharp and hardworking young woman who hasn't had the chance to learn the right approach yet."

"Well, that certainly sounds better than the ginormous failure label," said Alexis.

"Way, way better!" said Mia. "Now, I have one more question for you: what do you think the point of negotiation is? What's it really about?"

Alexis thought for a moment. "Well…it's about coming out ahead of the other person, isn't it? About making more money from the deal than they do? Or making them give you more than you're giving them? Oh, and I've heard it's about compromise, too, but you still want to make them compromise more than you do, right?"

"Do those feel like the right answers to you?"

Alexis sighed. "I mean, not really. Like, those are the goals everyone talks about… or at least the ones Jorge and everyone around him talk about. But that's how they get into the whole be aggressive all the time thing, and that just doesn't feel like me. So, maybe they're not the point…but if not, what is?"

"Now that, my friend, is a great question. And it's one of the questions we'll explore together if you'd still like to work with me."

Alexis gasped. "You mean you still want to help me?"

Mia laughed again. "Of course I do! You remind me of me twenty years ago. I'd love to help you master negotiation. I only have one condition."

"What's that?"

"Like Mr. Miyagi in the old Karate Kid movie, I will promise to teach you…if you promise to learn. You must do whatever I tell you to do, even if it feels weird or backward or counterintuitive or even unrelated to negotiation. You can ask questions to clarify, but not to argue. Will that work for you?"

Alexis took a deep breath, then nodded. "Yes, I'll do it."

"Good!" said Mia. "Now, your first assignment is to go back to the other morning with Lucas. I want you to take the questions I asked you about how you were feeling during that meeting and ask yourself each of them at least a dozen times. We'll meet again in two days, and by then, I want you to be able to tell me exactly what you were feeling, at what exact moments you were feeling it, and why you were feeling it. Is that clear?"

Alexis's eyes were wide. "You want me to…keep reliving that horrible meeting? Really?"

Mia raised an eyebrow. "Was that an argument?"

"No! No, sorry," Alexis blurted. "I'll do it. It will probably be awful, but I'll do it."

"It will be awful, yes," said Mia gently. "But you still need to do it. And the day after tomorrow, I'll tell you why."

"Okay," said Alexis, wondering how she would make it through the next two days without a breakdown. This had better be worth it, *she thought.*

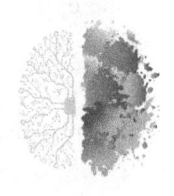

Chapter 1

WHY EVERYONE SUCKS
AT NEGOTIATION
(EVEN IF THEY DON'T THINK THEY DO)

"Let us never negotiate out of fear. But let us never fear to negotiate."
Inaugural address, January 20, 1961
—John F. Kennedy

I f you're reading this, you are probably terrible at negotiating.

How does that statement make you feel? Take a moment and connect with what comes up as you read the statement again.

You might be skeptical, upset, or angry at me. You might feel guilty or ashamed. Or you may simply feel confused, unsure, or uneasy.

Regardless of the way you feel, when you read that statement, you experienced emotions. In fact, I wrote that first statement specifically to trigger your emotions.

Why? Because negotiation is all about handling emotions in the moment. And how you're used to handling your emotions is why you probably suck at negotiating.

You can be a *skilled* negotiator in terms of mastering structure and methodology. You can be an *experienced* negotiator because you've done it many

21

times. You can even be a *lucky* negotiator who has managed to come out on top more often than not.

But none of those things help you navigate the minefield of emotions—which means that when those emotions come up in a negotiation, you're unprepared to handle them.

Negotiation isn't about skills or knowledge, it's about being able to perform under stress, while you experience emotions.

It's kind of like driving on a racetrack vs. on a normal highway.

You know how to drive your car on the street or the highway. So, racing may look easy from the outside—it's just driving in a big circle, right?

But from the inside of the racecar, it is really hard! On the racetrack, you have no time to think, you're in a very high-stress situation, and any small mistakes or misperceptions can get you seriously injured. When you take a curve or a turn at 150 mph, there are G forces that would bruise you if you tried to stand against them. Racecars are built with doors that don't open because if your door flew open in the middle of a race, you'd fly out of the car!

How do you become a racecar driver? It takes a lot of practice, confidence, and a strong ability to manage stress, follow your strategy, and adapt at any given point in time if the race doesn't go as planned. In addition to these skills, you need to be calm and in control enough to slow down your thoughts, handle your emotions, and expand your field of view, providing you with more options if needed.

It is the same with negotiation: You may be a good negotiator when it's easy, when you have more power than the other side, when the terms are simple, etc. But like driving at 150 mph, how do you drive your negotiation when it's not going as planned, when it goes too fast and you need to pivot quickly, or when it feels like you are about to hit a wall?

When we are emotional, we feel out of control, like someone else has taken over our body and mind. We may feel like things are moving at the speed of light, beyond our ability to react, or that everything (including ourselves) has slowed to a crawl, so every painful detail is crystal clear. Emotion wrecks our judgment, our creativity, and our ability to stand up for ourselves—so most of the decisions we make while emotional are bad ones.

So, trying to negotiate (or drive) from that standpoint just doesn't work. This is why most of us are so awful at negotiation.

The good news is it isn't entirely our fault. It's usually because of how we're taught to negotiate in the first place.

There are three inherent reasons many of us negotiators suck: we're told never to acknowledge our emotions, we're taught money is more important than emotion, and we think we're good enough without handling our emotions. In this chapter, we'll look at each of these myths.

Myth One: Never Show Weakness

We've all learned early on in our careers that to be successful in business, especially when managing people and climbing the corporate ladder, that being emotional makes us look weak. In the western world, you work hard to control your emotions, to be able to bend under pressure but never break. You aim to always be in control…even when your instinctual reaction is fight or flight.

But emotions don't like to be controlled, and more often than we'd like to think, they end up taking over a situation we intended to handle calmly and rationally.

Negotiation is a paradox—it's both the situation where you want to be the *most* calm and rational, and the situation where the *most* emotion comes up. You all know how challenging it is to make decisions when you are *emotional*… but what you don't realize is how *emotionally attached* you are in almost every negotiating situation.

Most "good" negotiators always seem to be in control—entirely without emotion, except maybe a bit of anger or passion. But what's really happening is they're trying to ignore, force down, or otherwise control the very real emotions they're experiencing—without ever showing it to the other side of the table. They might seem to be in control on the surface, but underneath, they are furiously treading water, spending a lot of effort and energy overriding their emotions.

The problem is that the price they pay to do that is *insane*. Every time you are emotional, your body secretes hormones that increase tension and stress. Your heartbeat accelerates, your breathing changes, and your muscles tense up. These hormones have one job—to get you to respond RIGHT NOW! So the amount of work your body has to do to override its natural responses, to show nothing but calm, is staggering—and it *hurts* you.

When you try to suppress strong emotions like fear and anger, it can feel like something is squeezing your heart. This makes sense because long-term suppression of emotions has been tied to heart attacks, burnout, and life-threatening diagnoses. (1) In the long run, trying to negotiate by suppressing our emotions doesn't work. We are human beings with feelings, and we can't control them or stop having them entirely. And trying not to show them literally damages our bodies and our health—that's how natural and normal emotions are.

For all of us, the challenge is that we overestimate our ability to deal with our emotions. We don't actually know how to manage them, but we tend to think we do. So, we either try to rationalize them (and pretend they don't really exist), we dread them (and try to force them down so we don't have to deal with them), or we just "wing it" (and hope they don't show up).

Have any of those methods worked for you? Did you ever rationalize with yourself that you could ignore, suppress, or dodge your emotions in a negotiation? Did it work? If it did, could you do it again under different circumstances?

Maybe. But I'm betting it wasn't easy.

What if you didn't have to choose between fighting a losing battle with your emotions and just let them take over? What if you could just be with them, where you felt them, but they didn't hurt or control you?

It's possible. This book is here to help you get there.

Myth Two: Negotiation is All About the Money

"What? Isn't negotiation *all* about money? How is that a myth? Are you crazy?"

Nope, I'm not crazy. Most people think negotiation is only about money, but it's not, at least not entirely. Money can be a factor in and an outcome of a negotiation, but it's not actually the main point or priority of negotiating.

How do I know this?

Because you can conclude a negotiation that gives you money and still be unhappy. You can also conclude one that *doesn't* give you money and be thrilled. In other words, you can make money and still feel like you've "lost" the negotiation or lose money and still feel like you've "won."

Part of this is because there are so many other things that can be included in negotiation terms besides money. But more of it is because money (and other possible items to haggle over) are only the surface of what's actually happening.

How often do you hear people say they are arguing or negotiating for the principle and not the money? Or how often do you see people get angry because they feel betrayed, ignored, or disrespected? And how often do you think you're making the best, most logical proposal to the other person, a proposal that's as financially beneficial for them as it is for you, yet they still refuse it?

On the surface, negotiation may *seem* to be about money, or at least about whatever the terms may include. But when you look deeper, negotiation is really about fears (fear of judgment, rejection, failure, incompetence, or looking bad) and desires (desire for respect, appreciation, inclusion, for a "win," or to save face).

And what's a word that encompasses both fears and desires? Emotions.

Emotions are forces in play on both sides of the table. If you don't stop and recognize them, you will miss a considerable part of the negotiation. On the other side of the table, you'll miss signals and cues that will help you understand what the other person wants and needs. On your side, you'll miss your body's natural warnings that things might not be as good as they seem. And on both sides, you'll miss opportunities to prevent disaster and/or turn a stressful moment into a win-win.

To illustrate this idea, I'd like to tell you about a time I missed out on negotiation success because I was solely focused on the money—and wasn't aware of or prepared to handle my own emotions.

Earlier in my career, while I was a VP of Global Sales, I had to renegotiate a contract with my company's biggest customer in China. This customer's account was paying a lower price than my company needed and was taking way too long to pay for the products they ordered. I needed to increase their rates by 10% and bring their payment terms from net 180 (paid within 180 days) to net 30 (paid within 30 days).

A price increase of 10% *and* a six-times-faster pay rate was a huge ask, especially for a single negotiation. Plus, this was right before the 2008 summer Olympic Games in Beijing, and everybody in China was under tremendous pressure to show the world how strong and professional China was. So, I knew the customer wouldn't just give me everything I wanted. But I felt like I had the skills to make it happen, and I wanted to prove myself as a good international negotiator by coming home with a win, so I decided to go for it.

I arrived in China in the morning, and sat down for the meeting that same afternoon, confident that I'd be back on my return flight in just a few hours with the new terms all set. And I felt the two-hour negotiation was going pretty well… until about 15 minutes before I needed to head to the airport. At that point, the customer's negotiator stopped talking, and his boss walked into the room.

The boss sat down in front of me and said, "We can't pay you in 30 days. We must have net 180 days like in the last contract." As I tried to explain the rationale for moving them to net 30, he responded aggressively that the *only* way this contract would move forward was if we kept the net 180 condition, and that if I couldn't promise that, he'd walk away from the contract immediately. Then for the remainder of the meeting, he glared at me with intense, angry eyes, as if he was daring me to make him walk away.

At this point, I was completely freaking out. Not only had my smooth negotiation gone off the rails, but I was now in danger of losing my company's biggest account in China—and I only had a few minutes to save the situation before I missed my flight home! In a rush of fear, I agreed to the net 180 request just to get the contract signed.

On my flight home, I reflected on what had happened. I'd gotten the 10% price increase I wanted, which meant I'd made my company more money…but I'd still failed in the negotiation. Not only had I missed a major objective, but I'd also caved under pressure, which I knew could create a tough precedent for future negotiations with that company. Plus, I hadn't explored other potential options (such as postponing the contract signing to take the customer's terms back to my boss and returning with a new proposal later) because, in my moment of panic when I felt things going out of control, I didn't even think of them.

This was one of the first moments I realized negotiation wasn't really about money. I hadn't caved because of money at all. I'd caved because I was afraid of my boss being angry at me for not bringing a deal home and having to pay for another business class ticket to China. I feared that he would see me as incompetent even after 18 months on the job. I felt I needed to prove myself to my boss and to our Chief Financial Officer. It was all about saving face for me.

I also realized in that moment that I wasn't as good at negotiation as I'd thought. When my counterpart's boss came in late in the meeting, demanding conditions and staring at me with angry eyes, it changed the dynamic in a way that I wasn't expecting—and it brought up emotions I wasn't prepared to deal with.

And that brings up another reason most of us suck at negotiation—we already think we're good at it.

Myth Three: But I'm Supposed to Be Good at This!

Here's the thing: rationally, you probably already know how to negotiate.

Maybe you studied it in school. Many business programs have negotiation as one of their classes, either mandatory or elective. So, if you have a business degree, you may feel like you've checked the negotiation box already. But do you remember what you took from that class? Have you practiced what you have learned since then? I have a couple of binders in my garage from the negotiation programs I have attended. I don't remember the last time I took them off the shelf. They are simply collecting dust.

Or maybe you've been trained in sales and gotten pretty good at it, so you think you know everything about negotiation. But like the college class, training that happened a while ago rarely creates a long-term impact. Unless you are regularly practicing with a coach or a mentor, training sessions rarely stick.

What if you got a promotion, a raise, or a great hiring package? Or if you had a few successful negotiations with clients in the past? That makes you a good negotiator, right? Well, maybe...but maybe not. You might have been in the right place at the right time, maybe the environment was favorable to you, or perhaps you had a product that nobody else had. It sounds counterintuitive but getting favorable outcomes in the past doesn't mean you'll get them in the future—or that your skills were the reasons you got them.

You might also be wondering what the big deal is. "Negotiation is simple," you might say, "you start high, they start low, you argue with the other person for a while, and then you meet somewhere in the middle where you both have to compromise. That's all there is to it." But is it really that simple? What happens when the arguing doesn't stop? What happens when the other side changes the dynamic on you the way my customer's boss did to me in China?

It's easy to think that you're already good at negotiation, and thus you don't have to work at it or dig below the surface level of money and compromise. You may want to write failed negotiations off as flukes or off days because you believe you're better than your results make you look. But if you're honest with yourself (as I had to be on that long flight home from China), you probably know you aren't as good as you think.

It's easy to get frustrated when negotiations don't go your way because you think you're *supposed* to be good at it—especially if any of the above scenarios are true for you. And I'll be honest—even if you aren't great at negotiation yet, you may be better than you think. If you aren't a top performer in your company, you didn't get a promotion, or you failed to keep a tough customer, that doesn't necessarily mean you're inherently lousy at the skill set of negotiation.

In other words, the fact that you probably suck at negotiation has nothing to do with how skilled or trained or experienced you are in *how to negotiate*. You may know those skills cold, or you may need to brush up on them, but what's really going on here is that you're letting your emotions around negotiation write your story for you.

If you think you're so good at negotiating that you don't need to practice or prepare or learn about the emotional side, your underlying story may be that you're afraid of admitting you aren't perfect or being afraid to look like you've failed.

If you think you're so terrible at it that practicing or preparing or learning about the emotional side won't be worth doing, your underlying story may be that you're afraid of being rejected or getting yelled at by someone who has power over you.

Maybe your stories aren't exactly like those, but the point is that one big reason so many of us suck at negotiation is that we've already let our fears take control before we even start. And the more we dread negotiating, the less we are willing to work on getting better at it, which leads to worse outcomes, which reinforces our fearful story around negotiation. The whole thing becomes a vicious circle.

But because this whole issue starts with an emotion in the first place—fear—the only way to get past it is to address the emotional side of negotiation.

Okay, so by now, you should be pretty clear on why not handling emotions makes it harder to succeed in negotiation. But where do these emotions come from? Why do we have to deal with them? And why do they come up so strongly when we negotiate?

In the next chapter, we'll answer those questions. (Here's a hint: the reason emotions are so troublesome is hidden in the title of this book.)

Exploration

1. What if your perception of your negotiation performance has nothing to do with the way you think about it? What if you can learn the true origin of that perception, manage it, and overcome it?

2. What is coming up for you as you read this question? What emotions do you feel right now?

3. What happens inside your body when a negotiation doesn't go as planned?

4. How would you describe your ability to maintain control in that situation and stay rational?

5. What stories do you tell yourself around your experiences with negotiation? What emotions are behind those stories?

Alexis Learns Her First Lesson

"So, are you ready to walk me through your meeting?" asked Mia. It was a bright Saturday morning, and she and Alexis were sitting on patio chairs on Mia's screened porch.

"As ready as I'm going to get," said Alexis. "You were right, by the way…going through it again was pretty awful."

"I know," said Mia. "But after today, you won't have to do it again—and you'll be in much better shape for the next meeting if it doesn't go as well as you hoped. Now, let's hear about your feelings in the meeting with Lucas."

Alexis took a deep breath and glanced at her notes. "Okay, so first of all, I was really nervous and anxious just going into the meeting. Like, I knew what I was supposed to say to Lucas, but I didn't feel comfortable saying it."

"Good," said Mia. "This anxiety, where did you feel it in your body?"

"In my stomach," Alexis said after a moment's thought. "My stomach was unsettled like I had bees in there instead of butterflies. I thought I might be sick, actually."

"Anywhere else?" asked Mia.

"In my hands and arms, I think. I couldn't seem to hold them still—they kept wanting to shake."

"Okay, excellent. What did you feel next?"

"I started feeling a bit more confident as I told Lucas what Jorge had told me to say. Everything was going okay, so my stomach relaxed a little, and some of the anxiety eased," Alexis said. "But then when I finished, and Lucas started asking me questions I thought he already knew the answers to, it all came rushing back, and I couldn't seem to stop talking."

"Understandable," said Mia. "Then what?"

"Then Lucas blew up at me! And my anxiety turned into full-on fear. I remember my heart started beating super-fast, and my breathing sped up, and I wanted to stand up to him like Jorge said, but I couldn't make myself move. I was literally scared stiff."

"Not an uncommon reaction when being yelled at," noted Mia. "After he finished shouting, what did you feel?"

"Still scared, only now it wasn't scared like running-from-a-bear, it was scared like oh-man-I-screwed-up. My stomach went from a buzzing beehive to an empty pit in about three seconds. All I could think was 'what am I going to tell Jorge; he's counting on me to renew this contract today.' It was like the rest of the world went gray for a minute, and that was the only thing I was aware of."

"Good," repeated Mia. "Anything else?"

"Well, I felt that same sense of apprehension, I think, all the way back to the office. And I started feeling ashamed, too. Like I should have known better, done better, heck, been better. Oh, and I should probably say I'm still feeling some of that, and some of it has morphed into feeling depressed over the last few days."

Mia nodded. "Very good, Alexis. You did this first exercise exactly as I hoped you would—you didn't hold back from those feelings at all."

"No, I sure didn't," said Alexis, "but I'm still not sure why that's a good thing."

"It's a good thing because the first step in a successful negotiation is being able to identify your feelings in the heat of the moment."

Alexis blinked. "Wait, what? I don't see the connection."

Mia grinned wryly. "That's because I haven't told you what the connection is yet. But I'm about to! Now tell me one more thing, Alexis: what do all of the feelings you felt during that meeting have in common, other than largely being negative ones and all taking place during the same meeting?"

Alexis thought about that one for a full minute before saying, "Um…this feels too obvious, but I guess that I was the one feeling them all?"

"Exactly!" Mia leaned forward excitedly. "During that meeting, if someone had hit the pause button and asked you how you were feeling, you'd have said 'I'm anxious,' 'I'm scared,' 'I'm ashamed.'"

"Well, yeah. I was feeling all of those things!"

"Ah, but were you really? Or were you listening to something that was telling you that you felt them?"

"You mean…like a voice in my head? I'm not crazy! Or at least I don't think I am!" Alexis snapped.

"No, of course not," said Mia reassuringly. "But hearing a voice in your head isn't crazy…when you believe that it's your own voice."

"I'm really not following you," said Alexis.

"Alright, let me try a different tack," said Mia. "What does the word 'ego' mean to you?"

"Um, well…ego is like someone's sense of themselves, right? Like if someone thinks a lot of themself, I'd say they have a big ego."

"Precisely," said Mia. "And everyone on Earth has an ego—a sense of themselves that tells them what they're feeling at any given moment. But the trick is that your ego doesn't sound like someone else telling you something. It sounds like—"

"My own voice talking inside my head!" Alexis cried. "That's what you meant about listening to a little voice in my head—it's not crazy, because as far as I'm concerned, it's just my own voice. And there's nothing crazy about my own voice being inside my head."

"Now you're getting it," said Mia. "But there's one more step to take. Do you, having made the breakthrough you just did, believe that your ego actually is your voice?"

Alexis bit her lip in thought. "Well…maybe? Like, I feel like the answer to that question should be no, but that feels weird just to say, you know? That the voice I hear in my head isn't my voice."

"It is a bit strange at first," agreed Mia. "But it's the key to cracking the code of successful negotiation. Once you can identify what your ego is telling you to feel, you can separate yourself from those feelings. Which means you don't have to feel them unless you choose to!"

"Wait a second," protested Alexis. "Are you telling me I didn't have to be paralyzed with fear when Lucas was shouting in my face? That I could have just chosen not to feel that way?"

"That's exactly what I'm telling you," said Mia. "Now, you're probably not ready to do that today, but rest assured: you will be in time. It's what I taught Jonathan and Kamal and dozens of other people to do, and it's what I'm going to teach you to do."

"Wow," said Alexis. "I can't believe I'll ever be able to do that."

"Don't worry about it right now," said Mia. "For the time being, I'll believe it for you."

Alexis grinned in relief. "Well, that should help!"

"Now, I'd like us to take a break for lunch. There's a fantastic bistro up the street, and for the next two hours, you're going to eat a nice, leisurely meal there."

"You're not coming with me?"

"Nope! I've already made my lunch here, and I have an assignment for you to do while you eat."

"Okay, if you say so," said Alexis. "What's the assignment?"

"I want you to examine the feelings you felt during the meeting with Lucas. Don't relive them this time! But look at them from the outside, as though they were sculptures under glass in a museum. Then as you look, ask yourself one question: why?"

"Why?"

"Yes, why. Why did my ego tell me to feel that particular feeling at that particular moment? Once you've finished eating and have some answers to that question, come on back here and we'll talk again."

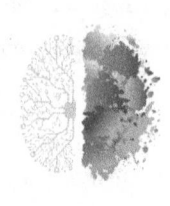

Chapter 2
THE LITTLE VOICE IN YOUR HEAD

"Your emotions make you human. Even the unpleasant
ones have a purpose. Don't lock them away. If you
ignore them, they just get louder and angrier."
—Sabaa Tahir

In my China negotiation example, I mentioned that I made a bad call because, in the moment, I was dealing with a huge rush of fear. But I wasn't afraid of the people across the table from me—not even the boss who was glaring at me so angrily. I was scared of my boss's reaction to my failure, and his evaluation and judgment about my performance. I wanted to look good to my boss—or at least save face when things went sideways. Why did I feel so much fear around my boss's reaction? My little voice was telling me that I was screwed if I didn't produce a result my boss liked.

What little voice?

The little voice we all have, the one that tells us when to be scared or angry or sad—the one that tells us "run!" or "fight back!" or "stand up for yourself!" or "surrender!" when something feels stressful.

This voice doesn't usually use words. But we recognize it in the emotions it stirs up in us whenever an external event triggers them.

Here's how the voice works: An event happens, and it triggers something in your brain. Your mind quickly searches your memories or survival blueprint to find the same situation or a similar one that happened in the past and grabs onto the first thing you think you should do in response. Then the voice tells your body to do that thing *right now*, and your body does it! And because it all takes place in a fraction of a second, it feels like an automatic reaction to the external event.

In China, the voice showed up to me as a frightened reaction to my customer's boss glaring at me: "just give him what he wants so you don't lose the client!" I don't remember ever thinking those exact words, but they were exactly what my little voice was telling me to do.

As Mia pointed out, there's a name for this little voice: the ego.

We All Have an Ego

Yes, you have an ego. So do I. Everyone does. If you meditate six hours per day or do a lot of spiritual work, your ego might play a smaller role in your life; for most people, the ego is very present and controlling—usually, it comes out as what most people call "their personality."

Having an ego is not a problem in itself. The problem arises when your ego tries to control you.

When the first humans evolved, ego was very helpful in developing survival instincts. Back then, a strong sense of self-preservation and self-interest could literally mean the difference between hunting a meal and *becoming* a meal. Your ego taking control of you was a good thing, because its split-second instructions to defend yourself or run away could literally save your life before your mind could process danger.

Nowadays, ego and its survival instinct are still useful when you face a life-threatening situation or a health crisis. But those aren't everyday situations the way they were in the Stone Age. Surviving a predator's attack or warding off starvation aren't common emergencies these days.

The problem is your ego comes from the deepest, oldest part of your brain—the part that first evolved when *all* of human existence was fight or flight and eat or be eaten.

So, when your ego can't find life-threatening situations to react to the way it did for hundreds of thousands of years in your ancestors' brains, it does the next best thing: *it makes them up*. When your ego tells you today to react, or tries to take control and make you react, chances are there's no actual danger to you.

Think about it. In today's world, you are bombarded with demands and expectations of highest-level performance. You find yourself continually managing conflicts with yourself and others. And periodically, you end up at a negotiation table. None of these scenarios are life-threatening, yet from the way your mind and body respond to them, they might as well be! Your ego interprets these daily situations as threats and instinctively puts you into a state of high alert—often without you even being aware of it.

This is where your emotions often come from. Your ego registers an external event that makes it feel threatened, excited, or otherwise agitated. Then it tells you that *you* are threatened, excited, or agitated. And because it uses your mind to do it (and speaks in the first person), you become threatened or excited, and your mind and body react accordingly.

Other than the emotions you felt as a newborn (before the ego developed), the majority of your emotions are ego-driven. When you feel or sense them, especially the negative ones, it's because your ego either didn't get what it was expecting or fears it won't.

Imagine the following situations:

- You are *angry* or *upset* because someone *didn't do what you expected or didn't behave the way you wanted them to.*
- You *are upse*t at your spouse because she didn't read you well or understand your *unspoken needs.*
- You are *excited* because you just got a promotion. You *feel* you deserve it because you are *better* than everyone else.
- You are preparing to negotiate, and you are *afraid* of losing the deal.
- You don't want to *upset* another person, so you are *not assertive* and clear about your *needs.*

All these emotions are a demonstration that your ego is in control. They show either an underlying desire to get what your ego wants, or an underlying fear that you won't get it.

From that perspective, emotions arise because they are the messengers from your ego to your body and mind, carrying crucial information for you and about you. Emotions are a source of energy, a defense mechanism, signaling about what your ego is going through. The stronger the emotions, the stronger their messages are and the harder your ego fights to take control.

nEGOtiation—When the Little Voice Takes Over the Table

Negotiation is always ego-driven. Both parties want something, and when it doesn't go as planned, their egos react. Emotions come up. Instinctual fight/flight/freeze/faint reactions take over. People lash out or shut down or just fail to think of anything other than what their ego is telling them.

Okay, so how did that show up in Alexis's meeting with Lucas?

To put it simply, Alexis's ego took over the whole process. Her ego felt threatened from the beginning—not only was she being asked to negotiate at a level she hadn't been trained for, but her status and her boss's approval were at risk if she failed. So, before she even scheduled the meeting, her ego was sending her waves of emotional fear—hence the anxiety she felt.

Then in the meeting itself, her ego perceived the customer's questions as a threat to her control of the situation, so she (partly unconsciously) resorted to a persuasive sales technique (repeating the terms of the proposal) to try and keep control and get the customer to do what she wanted. We didn't explore his side of things, but Lucas was likely also in his ego after not feeling heard when asking his questions about cost increase and predictability—not to mention being upset that Alexis's company decided to pull the plug on a contract extension so suddenly!

Finally, in response to a much more aggressive threat from the customer, Alexis's ego went into full reaction mode and shut down her ability to respond.

In hindsight, it's easy to understand that for both sides, ego-driven emotions showed up because neither were getting what they wanted. Their logical approaches to negotiating got derailed once their egos took over.

Alexis's ego prevented her from discussing another option with her boss around the contract extension. Her ego was taking control when she went into persuasion with the customer to prove herself and keep control. And her ego was in full protection mode when she pulled back and couldn't respond to the customer's angry demands.

Alexis mentioned when talking to Jorge that she wished she'd had more negotiation training. That might have helped, but because we know that emotions took over the conversation on both sides, the reality is Alexis needed to be aware of her ego and trained or coached on how to deal with it, which most negotiation training wouldn't cover. Because she wasn't aware of her ego controlling her and the situation, she couldn't see any way around what was happening—and better negotiation skills wouldn't have saved her.

So how do you avoid falling into that trap? How do you become aware of your ego? And once you're aware of it, how do you deal with it so it doesn't control you in stressful moments like negotiations?

First, you must grasp the one simple truth Mia helped Alexis to understand: *you are not your ego.*

Your Ego Is Not You!

Wait, what?

I know that sounds weird and confusing. But remember at the top of this chapter, when I first talked about the ego? I didn't call it "me" or "I." I called it "the little voice we all have." A little voice telling us things in our heads *isn't the same as our actual selves.* Your ego is different and separate from you.

The problem is, your ego uses your voice, so it *sounds* exactly like you. Your ego doesn't say, "you need to protect yourself!" It says, "*I* need to protect *myself.*" It doesn't say "*you* want that!" it says, "*I* want that!" If you look at the origin of the word "ego" ("ego" is Latin for "I"), it shows that your ego wants you to think it's you, because that way you will act in its best interests—thinking they're *your* best interests. It wants to control you. That's why in stressful situations, it often looks and feels like you have no other choice but to react—because your ego is literally trying to take control of your mind and body.

And because most of us aren't even aware we have an ego, let alone how it tries to control us, the vast majority of the time, we drift into an automatic, mostly unconscious state of reaction where we have no control at all over ourselves. We act and react at the direction of our egos, almost like puppets who can only move if someone else pulls their strings.

But your ego is not the real you. It is your learned personality, a construct of many beliefs and experiences that started to develop when you were growing up.

Ego is not the real you. It's your developed personality.

I came from a family where the image and opinion of others were and still are the main drivers of individual self-worth, including my own. From that ego conditioning, I learned to behave in a way that people would appreciate me better, love me, recognize me. The best way for my ego to get what it wanted was to become a people pleaser, search for their approval, and avoid upsetting them.

But as I grew older and more established in my career, I began to realize that my people-pleasing ways were actually hurting me! The very people I thought would like and approve of me because of that behavior started telling me they couldn't trust me. They saw me as a fake, a brown-noser, a yes-man. They didn't want a colleague who only told them what they wanted to hear and couldn't stand up for himself. I had to face the fact that what my ego wanted me to do wasn't healthy or helpful—and learn that if I didn't like myself first, no amount of people-pleasing would get other people to do it for me.

There are two points to take away here. First, your ego isn't evil. It's trying to protect you, make sure you're accepted, and get you the feelings of love and safety you had when you were an infant. But it only knows one way to do that: to take control of you and make you do what it wants. And what it wants isn't always the best option for you.

Second, you can overcome your ego and choose to do something other than what it tells you! You may think that you are who you are, with no room for growth or change. But the truth is that you can choose *not* to let your ego control or define you. Your ego warps your sense of reality, offering a distorted image of the true you by masking it with a surface-level personality. But you don't *have* to fall for it. You have a choice.

A big step in making that choice is recognizing your emotions—the messengers of your ego—for what they really are: *information*.

Emotion = Information

Your emotions, for the most part, are a response to your ego. Your emotions are not who you are; they are simply a part of you.

The reason you experience emotions is that *they represent a source of information that you should pay attention to.* Remember how ego first developed in humans as a sense of self-preservation? Being aware that you are scared because you are facing a hungry lion or another life-threatening situation is part of your survival blueprint. That sense of fear *gets your attention right away so you can respond in time to survive.*

Being aware that you are afraid of failing or angry at someone for rejecting you provides the same crucial *information* for you to pay attention to *right now*, but what that information shows you isn't an immediate threat to your survival. If you are willing and able to see it that way, you can take in the information without letting it force a negative reaction in your mind.

Let's look at the information Alexis's emotions gave her at the beginning of this book. Alexis felt powerless after the meeting with her boss because she *didn't express her need for reassurance* by asking if there were any alternative solutions. She saw the customer's questions about her proposal as *questioning her competence*, and she took the customer's angry proposal rejection as *a personal rejection*. In all three cases, the emotions she experienced—anxiety, indignation, fear—were sources of information about something not matching up with her expectations and what that mismatch meant to her.

Unless you are a newborn, emotions are not who you are.

They are your personality, your ego—and can give you information you might not have now.

Whenever I felt angry when I was younger, I used to run away from the anger or pretend that I was not upset. In my family, being angry was perceived as a source of disrespect and a lack of self-control. I was afraid that if I expressed my anger, I would get in trouble. So, I ran from it, pretended it wasn't there, and pushed back against it so it wouldn't control me.

As I grew up, though, my feelings of anger got stronger, and my threshold for feeling them got lower. Every day it became more challenging to hide or suppress the anger, but I didn't feel like I had any other options for managing it. I started to be afraid I might explode and hurt someone emotionally or physically.

Fortunately, I discovered personal growth work, which gave me new tools and perspectives to confront and understand my anger. I began to appreciate it for what it really was: a marker that something was not working inside of me.

I would feel anger when someone wouldn't or couldn't guess what I wanted or needed. I would be angry at traffic because I had expectations about the time to get where I wanted to go, and it wasn't going as planned. I'd feel it towards team members who weren't doing their share of work but would still take credit as part of the team. I would get angry at people lying to me because I felt disrespected.

The minute I understood that my anger was a signal that something inside of me wasn't aligned, I stopped running away from it and started to be curious about its meaning.

This is what it means to see emotion as information. Emotions tell us things about ourselves that we can't always see or understand through logic and intellect. They tell us deep, secret things and desperate, urgent things; things we know but don't know we know. Most of all, they tell us what our ego is reacting to and why it wants us to embrace that reaction.

- If you are experiencing anger, it may be a sign that your needs, desires, expectations are not being fulfilled.
- If you compare yourself with others or blame others, it may be a sign that you don't like a part of yourself.
- If you buy a bigger house and a more expensive car than you need, it may be a sign that you're trying to prove your worth to others (or to yourself)

These are the kinds of information your emotions give you clues about. If you ignore them, your ego will continue to manifest itself with even stronger emotions, and you will get more and more emotional around the same issues.

Most of the ways we as human beings try to handle our emotions end up making them worse. Let's look at three big ones:

1. Choosing not to have emotions / "turning the switch off." Okay, you can pretend that you have no emotions...but you are human, and feelings are part of life. It's not an option to feel nothing. Emotions are always present—and by suppressing them, you're missing out on all the helpful information they give you. This leads to a dangerous lack of self-knowledge, which can fuel years of pain and futility.

2. Ignoring them/shutting them out. This tends to happen when we're willing to feel our emotions, but then try to control them by being logical and rational. The problem is, we feel emotions in our bodies—which means that even if we try to keep them out of our minds, they will still manifest physically. Not only does this lead to pressure, stress, tension, or numbness in the body, but it also leads to unconscious body language that can easily be read from across a negotiation table. Plus, if you fight them for control like I used to do with anger, you may win in the short term, but the emotion will just come back stronger later on.

3. Letting them control you/identifying with them. This is essentially giving in to your ego and allowing it to take over your sense of self. Whatever your ego says about you, that's how you think of yourself, so whenever your ego tells you to react emotionally, that's exactly what you do. But as we've seen, your ego doesn't work in your best interest. Identifying yourself as your ego and your emotions can lead to feeling justified in losing control and hurting people, feeling like you deserve to be bullied or intimidated, or feeling like everything is your fault—or that nothing is—because that's "just the way you are."

In my example earlier in this chapter, I came to understand that I was angry because I was identifying with the anger as part of myself. I thought I was "an angry person." And that made fighting back or running away from my anger really difficult because I felt like I was fighting or running from myself. In reality, I'm not an angry person. Yes, at times I do feel anger, and I understand that I need to embrace and learn from that anger, but the feeling itself doesn't define who I am.

There's a better way to deal with emotions. You don't have to pretend they don't exist, try to shove them down, or just give up and let them take over. Instead, you can be aware of them, treat them as information, and use them to your benefit—even in the heat of the moment in a negotiation meeting. In the next chapter, we'll look at how to do this and why it works so well.

Explorations

1. After reading this chapter, what emotions are coming up for you? What is your ego telling you to do? Be curious and try to understand why you are reacting the way you are.

2. Take a sheet of paper and draw three columns at equal distance from each other.

In the left column, write this statement:
I feel better, superior to others; I deserve it because…

In the column in the middle of the sheet, write this statement:
I feel inferior, deficient to others, I need to be seen and heard, I need to prove myself, or I feel like a victim because…

In the right column, write this statement:
I feel like everybody else, average, not unique in any way because…

Take your time to come up with your answers. Make sure you include at least 3-5 statements in each quadrant.

What is going on inside of you?

Which emotions are rising?

What is your ego telling you?

Do you see a trend, a pattern?

Do you have a column with many statements?

Why do you think that is?

What did this exercise show you about your ego?

Alexis Explores Her Own Mind

"So, really, I was feeling all those feelings because my ego felt threatened," finished Alexis. "It told me to be nervous about the outcome of the meeting because my career was riding on it, it told me to be so anxious I couldn't shut up because something had to be wrong, it told me to be scared because I was getting yelled at, and it told me to be ashamed and depressed because I was a ginormous failure. Is that right?"

"Do you think it is?" asked Mia.

"I…yes, I do," said Alexis. "But I still don't see how I could have understood that in the moment—when I couldn't even think—or even how understanding it could have changed how I felt."

"The answer to the first question is that this level of self-awareness is a skill like any other. It can be learned, mastered, and ultimately practiced very quickly—even as your ego is telling you you're too scared or too angry or too ashamed to think straight."

"And the second question? What's its answer?"

"You already know part of it: that understanding what your ego is telling you to feel allows you to observe it from the outside, without having to feel it. What you don't yet know, but we're about to cover this afternoon, is that doing so opens up pathways and options you couldn't have thought of without first observing the ego and its emotional messengers in that way."

"Alright," said Alexis. "How does that work?"

"Are you familiar with the concept of mindfulness?"

"You mean like meditation?" asked Alexis. "Kamal and Ling do that a lot…I tried for a few days, but I kept dozing off."

"Not exactly, no. Meditation can help improve mindfulness, but they're not the same thing. Mindfulness is simply the practice of being aware of what's happening in your mind right now, what your ego is telling you to feel and do."

"And doing that gives me more options? Just being aware that I'm scared gives me the option not to be scared?" Alexis wondered aloud.

"It's the first step on that path, yes," said Mia. "I want you to think about driving your car at 95 miles per hour. How well would you react to another car pulling out in front of you when you're driving that fast?"

"Terribly!" said Alexis. "I'd probably hit them—or swerve really fast and hit someone else."

"Why?"

"Well, because I was going too fast to react safely or stop in time."

"Exactly. Now imagine the same scenario, but you're only driving 15 miles per hour. How would it be different?"

"I'd have a lot more time to respond and weigh my options. Like, I'd probably see the car a lot sooner, and then I could see if it made sense to turn or change lanes or just hit my brakes."

"Good. Now think of the practice of mindfulness like the brakes in your car. Your ego wants to drive at 95 miles per hour all the time, which means you feel like you only have one option: to do what it tells you. But mindfulness can slow down the car in your mind, so to speak, so you have more time to find other options and choose a better one.

"When you are mindful, it's as though you have a coach sitting with you in the room, speaking to you about the process in front of you, and advising you how to do it. This coach helps you see things you might not see on your own, asks you what you really want, helps you let go of things that don't matter. The only difference is that the coach is you, and the coaching happens at the speed of conscious thought."

"That sounds awesome!" exclaimed Alexis. "How do I make that happen?"

"Just like you learn anything else," said Mia. "You practice. Let's try an exercise right now. Close your eyes, please."

"Okay, I'm game," said Alexis, letting her eyelids fall closed.

"Put yourself back in the room with Lucas for a moment," instructed Mia. "But this time, don't focus on how your ego wanted you to feel. Keep yourself outside of the emotions. Observe them, notice them, but don't get caught up in them. With me so far?"

"Yes, I'm there," said Alexis.

"Now, I want you to think of at least three other things you could have done in response to Lucas getting upset with you, besides sitting there and just letting him yell, assuming the paralyzing fear didn't have full control of your body at the time."

Alexis was quiet for a moment. "Well, I could have yelled back at him."

"Yes, you certainly could have. What else?"

"I could have asked for a break to give him a chance to cool off and me a chance to get my thoughts together again."

"Absolutely. And third?"

"I could have, um…maybe I could have called Jorge? Or at least told Lucas I was just telling him what my boss told me to say?"

"Excellent," said Mia. "You can open your eyes now. How do you feel about those three options?"

"I don't like the first one. I'm not a shouter," said Alexis. "The third option might have worked with Lucas, but it might have gotten me in trouble with Jorge, too. So, I'm not sure about that. I like the second one, though. That might have been worth a try."

"I'd agree with you on all three. To be fair, having other options doesn't always mean having other GOOD options, at least not right away. But tell me, if you'd had more time, do you think you could have come up with three more possibilities?"

"Actually, yeah," said Alexis slowly, sounding a bit surprised. "I think I could have."

"So, when mindfulness allows you to slow down the pace of your ego, it gives you the time you need to think of those options. And by practicing mindfulness outside of high-stress situations, you can eventually master it enough so it will show up in those situations on its own."

"That makes sense," said Alexis. "But there's got to be some kind of catch here, right?"

"Oh, yes," Mia laughed. "The catch is that you have to DO the practice! Mindfulness isn't something you master overnight. It's a skill, like playing the cello or throwing a curveball or making a perfect apple pie. The more you do it, the better you get at it…and the less you do it, the more you stay where you are now."

"Okay, so I need to practice, sure," said Alexis. "But my next meeting with Lucas is in ten days! That can't possibly be enough time to master mindfulness, can it?"

"No, likely not," said Mia. "But don't worry. The goal of this next meeting won't be to close the deal."

"It won't?"

"Not yet. This meeting's goal will be to buy you more practice time. Don't worry. You'll be ready."

"Okay, if you say so," said Alexis. "What's my next assignment?"

"For the next three days, practice being aware of what you're feeling five times a day. Then when you have that awareness, ask yourself why you're feeling the way you are—and if that feeling might be from your ego. Sound good?"

"Yes, I can do that," said Alexis, standing and grabbing her bag and coat. "I'll call you in three days, then."

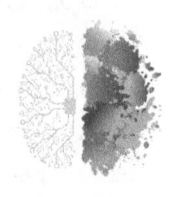

Chapter 3
THE ANSWER YOU'VE BEEN LOOKING FOR

"Mindfulness means being awake. It means knowing what you are doing."
—Jon Kabat-Zinn

What is mindfulness? Mindfulness is focusing your attention, in a compassionate and nonjudgmental way, to witness your experience in this minute, from the little voice in your head, the emotions you feel, to the sensations in your body.

This definition may sound a lot like a similar term, "presence." But there's an important difference between presence and mindfulness.

Presence focuses on what you are currently *doing*.

Let's say you are giving a presentation, acting in a play, or playing in a soccer game. In each of these situations, you are present, because you're fully focused on the activity you're performing. You're not on autopilot or performing mechanically; you're bringing your full self to whatever you're doing. That's presence. And you can be present without being mindful.

Mindfulness is the ability to observe and be curious about *what is going on inside of you.* If you're giving a presentation, you may be afraid of how your customer will respond. If you're acting in a play, you may be excited because it's opening night. If you're playing in a soccer game, you may be angry because you missed a goal. Mindfulness is what allows you to be aware of those feelings as they come up, then to slow down the speed of your mental process, so you have space and clarity to make the right decision in response to them.

To be clear, mindfulness is not the same as thinking. Instead, it's stepping back from your ego and its emotional messages to be aware and curious about your inner world. Mindfulness is also not the same as meditation, energy healing, astrology, crystals, or any other new-age practice. You don't have to go to Bali to be mindful (though you can certainly be as mindful in Bali as anywhere else!).

Mindfulness actually has its roots in neuroscience. In the last 20 years, the emergence of Functional Magnetic Resonance Imaging (fMRI) technology has allowed researchers to understand more clearly which part of the brain is responsible for which activities.

Are Three Brains Better Than One?

Neuroscience has discovered there are three parts of the brain that determine how you respond to external stimuli.

1. The reptilian brain is the oldest, earliest-evolved portion of your brain, located at its base. This part is responsible for self-preservation and instinctual responses. Its primary responsibility is to help you identify if a situation is a threat or not. If you are familiar with a situation, your reptilian brain sees it as less threatening and doesn't trigger a reaction. But if you are unfamiliar with what is coming up, the reptilian brain interprets it as threatening and, within a fraction of a second, triggers your survival reaction. This puts your body and mind into the fight-or-flight response.

2. The mammalian or limbic brain (amygdala) evolved after the reptilian brain and is located above it in your brainstem. This part of the brain is responsible for your instinctual emotional responses. The primary responsibility of this portion of the brain is to quickly assess and judge if you are in a good or bad situation.

3. The frontal lobe (neocortex) is responsible for intellectual and executive functions, conscious thinking, and self-awareness. Its primary function is

to examine what is happening externally, without emotional attachment from the past and your instinctual response.

The reptilian and limbic brains are fast movers—so fast, in fact, that we register their activity as unconscious or instinctive. They don't *think* so much as *react*. This worked well thousands of years ago when split-second reaction meant the difference between life and death, but these days they can get us into trouble because they don't differentiate between a real life-threatening situation and one that only *feels* threatening. As you'll remember from the last chapter, your ego lives in these parts of your brain.

The frontal lobe moves more slowly—this is where actual, conscious *thought* happens. It's where we try to be rational about our experiences. It's also where we can be *mindful* of them.

During functional MRI scans, subjects showed increased reptilian and mammalian brain activity when shown threatening images and asked how the images made them *feel*. On the other hand, when asked to *think* about a specific situation, for example their last vacation or last family reunion, the subjects showed increased frontal lobe activity.

That is one of the main reasons why mediation works so well. Good mediators will help their clients slow down and use their frontal lobe to express how they feel, rather than get triggered by the fast-moving reptilian and mammalian portions of their brains. This prevent the clients' egos from taking control. As you'll see shortly, this practice of helping the brain slow down to avoid knee-jerk ego control is also why mindfulness works so well in negotiation.

What Does Mindfulness Do?

Okay, so neuroscience helps us understand the back-end workings of mindfulness, but what does mindfulness actually *do* for us?

Mindfulness allows the frontal lobe of your brain to observe the world for what it is, without reacting to a real or imagined threat. Mindfulness tells your reptilian and limbic brains that you are okay, you're in control, there is no actual threat. Most importantly, mindfulness allows you to slow down in the moments when your instinctual emotional responses are triggered, it feels like you are not in control anymore, and everything starts moving way too fast.

Think about the NASCAR driver again. When they are "in the zone," everything seems to be in slow-motion, their reaction time speeds up, and they can make quicker decisions without doubting themselves. Their perspective is much bigger, and they can see the entire track in front of them. It's almost like they are observing themselves driving their cars. (Interestingly enough, studies have shown that the most stressful moments for a NASCAR driver are the fifteen-second pit stops—the times when they *aren't* driving!)

Being in the zone in negotiation means that you can slow down time and expand your vision of the situation the same way a NASCAR driver does on the track. You can see beyond your own emotions (and your opponent's), you can see the entire situation, you can be creative and access choices that you couldn't see otherwise. Ultimately, you can always know which option is the appropriate one to make in that specific situation.

Several studies have demonstrated that mindfulness leads to better performance:

- Fewer errors and higher emotional acceptance (Teper 2013)[1]
- Better present moment awareness and stronger acceptance of feelings (Cardaciotto 2008)[2]
- Better logic, reason, and thoughtful thinking (Schmeichel 2013)[3]
- Expanded working memory, more mental flexibility, and stronger resistance to instinctual responses (Caseda 2019)[4]

These studies prove mindfulness lets you maintain clarity under stress, build self-control that can combat the control of your ego, think rationally while experiencing emotion, pivot quickly, experience empathy and curiosity even in difficult conversations, and keep the positive belief that there is a workable solution in even the most heated negotiations.

Here's an example of how that can look.

Negotiating in Japan

My first truly mindful negotiation experience was when I went to Japan to renegotiate an agreement with all of my Japanese customers in the room at the same time. (I was still with the same company as in my China story, only a few years later.) We were coming off two back-to-back three-year agreements with these customers, without any price increases. In fact, the last price increase had been by 2%, nine years prior. My company felt that a price increase was long overdue.

Internally, we wanted to increase pricing by 16.5%, with our walk-away point set at 12.9%. We had all the data to support the workability of these numbers. We sat down with our local rep to make sure he understood our position. We sent our proposal in advance to give them time to review it, as I knew we probably couldn't close the negotiation in one meeting. (Per their request, it was a proposal for all of the Japanese customers, regardless of their size or growth rate.) In other words, my team and I were as ready for this negotiation as we could be.

The day of the meeting, I met with all our customers' executives, with my local Japanese sales representative on my side of the table to translate and advise. The executives all spoke English but preferred to negotiate in Japanese with my rep translating for me (this is a common business practice in Japan). For the first 90 minutes of the two-hour meeting, the customers asked me personal questions to get to know me better. Was I married? Did I have kids? What motivated me to accept my position as VP of Global Sales? I'd expected this—in Japan, no one does business with you until they know you personally, and this was my first visit there.

As we approached the last 30 minutes of the meeting, I indicated to my local rep that it was time to transition to business and made my proposal for the 12.9% price increase. The Japanese customers began sharing their logic on how the cost of living in Japan had been declining for the last several years. They all made statements on how difficult it would be to pass a cost increase to their customers at this time, and that it would take time to prepare their customers for any price increase, especially one as large as we were asking for. Eventually, they proposed a price increase of 10%. With only a few minutes left before I had to leave for the airport, my rep immediately and urgently whispered to me that we should accept their offer.

During the entire meeting, I had been very present and mindful of what was coming up for me. I was aware of getting impatient after 90 minutes of small talk and wishing my rep would hurry things up and get to business already. I was mindful of my calmness as they went through their reasoning around the declining costs of living. I was also aware of feeling manipulated and pressured as the customers tried to use time in their favor by proposing a price we couldn't accept at the very last moment of the meeting—and of feeling betrayed by my rep, who knew very well that 10% was unacceptable but was urging me (in front of the customers!) to accept it anyway.

In that moment, it was very tempting for my ego to take over. I felt a surge of frustration toward the customers and a flood of anger toward my rep for throwing me under the bus. I also felt the crunch of pressure—as with the China situation a few years earlier, I'd flown halfway around the world and really didn't want to fly back empty-handed. If I'd been the same person I was back then, I probably would have accepted the 10% increase just to come out with some kind of deal.

Instead, I took a deep breath, looked inward at what I was feeling, and felt time slow down so that each second almost felt like ten. Despite all the emotions I felt, I was very grounded and calm. My senses heightened, and I was aware of everything (even noticing a slight wind draft moving the curtains in the room).

I realized I didn't have to take the customers' manipulative tactics or my rep's recommendation as personal. The situation had nothing to do with me. So, I did not need to feel anger or frustration about it. All I needed to do was my job.

I stood, bowed slightly with my hands together in front of me, and informed the customers that I couldn't accept their offer—not only was the price not workable, but I would lose face with my company if I accepted. My rep's face turned red as he translated. Still, even before the translation was complete (remember, all the customers understood English), the most senior customer sitting next to the wall, near the door (he hadn't said a word the entire meeting, listening to every word I spoke to identify where I had flexibility) cut him off, saying "I think we should stop this conversation before it becomes unfriendly."

Soon after, I was on my way back to the airport with no deal in place. But I never felt stressed or out of control. I was clear with my intent and able to emotionally detach myself from the situation without losing respect for the people in front of me. I was mindful of my own emotions and never took anything personally.

Back in the office in North America, when I debriefed the meeting with my boss and the head of finance, I discovered I was the first person from my company not to cave to this group of customers. Nobody had ever walked away from that tactic without giving in. The Japanese customers couldn't believe I didn't show flexibility at the last minute, especially once my local rep had recommended, I take the deal. I think everybody lost face in that meeting, and I can't imagine what was discussed after I left.

As we reviewed the meeting, I remembered what the customers had said about needing time to let their clients know about the upcoming price increase. Based on that need, my boss and I crafted a different proposal that gave us the price increase we wanted, but over two years rather than immediately. I sent this revised proposal to my sales rep, asking him to let our customers know that I had heard them and created this counterproposal which took their needs consideration. We ultimately signed the new contract two months later, with that revised proposal as the cornerstone of the deal.

By Being Mindful in Negotiation, You Can Change the Outcome for Good.

There is no way I would have been able to stay present and in control with such a level of clarity without being mindful at every single moment of this negotiation. I felt like a monk negotiating, not reacting to their emotions or mine. (To give you an idea of how it could have gone, my rep was so far in his ego that he didn't communicate with our customers for three weeks after that meeting.)

If you compare this story with my China story in Chapter 1, you can see the difference between one negotiation where my emotions and fears took control of me and prevented me from being in control of the situations, and one where

I used mindfulness to defeat my ego and know what the right move was in the moment.

Given those kinds of results, you may be wondering: if mindfulness is so awesome, why doesn't everyone do it?

Well, …mostly because we don't want to.

Everyone Has an Excuse

The problem with mindfulness is that it doesn't happen automatically. We have to choose it, practice it, and build it into our mental processes. And let's be honest, that sounds a lot like work. We've already got work to do—often a lot of it! So, as human beings, our typical response to mindfulness is to find excuses not to do it. Here are a few of the big ones:

- **It's hard!**

Maybe you tried being mindful, and you were only able to do it for a few seconds (or not at all). Or maybe it just sounds too tough, and you think you won't be able to do it. There's nothing wrong with thinking that…but it means that your ego is still in control, likely bringing up struggles from the past and worries about the future to keep you from focusing on the present moment. Being mindful isn't actually that hard—but it does require some energy and effort at the beginning, just like learning any new skill. The good news is that the more you do it, the easier it gets.

- **I don't have time.**

I get it, you're busy. Learning a new skill does take time, and you've got a thousand and one other job tasks to do. But once you learn how to do it, being mindful will actually *save* you time. Think about it: If you have bad news to deliver and you're in your ego around it, you'll most likely hesitate and delay delivering it out of fear, drag out the leadup to make sure they're in a good mood first, spend extra time over-explaining to keep them from being upset, etc.

But if you realize you're scared and mindfully handle that fear, you'll be able to both prepare for the meeting more easily, take less time delivering the news, and devote *more* time to moving forward positively afterward.

- **I've always been like this, and nothing has fixed it. Why bother trying mindfulness?**

Remember when I talked about how I thought of myself as an angry person? I believed that was just how I was, and nothing could change it—I'd tried everything! But when I eventually learned mindfulness, it helped me see my anger in a new light. I understood it wasn't actually *me*; it was my ego trying to pass itself off as me. I wasn't an angry person by nature, I simply experienced anger just like everyone else did—which meant I wasn't fated or doomed to be controlled by it anymore.

I understand how easy it can be to feel like "this is just how I am; I can't change." But whether you think you're inherently angry, afraid, timid, unworthy, impatient, arrogant, or anything else, I promise you that isn't you. It's only your ego, and your ego is not you. Since mindfulness is the only thing I know which can defeat ego, it's worth at least giving it a try.

- **I have way too many things to pay attention to. If I focus on mindfulness, I'll miss something important—and maybe screw up my work.**

This one is understandable because our lives are overflowing with things trying to grab our attention. We live in a constant state of FOMO (fear of missing out), where by doing one thing, we automatically worry about the ten things we *aren't* doing. Our jobs don't help with this, as they typically expect us to multitask constantly (even though every study on multitasking has shown it actually makes us *less* productive).

Where do you think these feelings of fear and anxiety come from? If you said, "my ego," you're right! Your ego wants to keep you in a constant state of fast motion—jumping from one thing to the next, worrying about the past and the future, trying to do everything at once—because speed and reaction are all it knows how to do. Your anxiety makes your ego feel safe, even as it leads to stress and tension that actively hurt your mind and body.

Mindfulness is about the present moment. Your ego is afraid of mindfulness, as it loses all its power when you are mindful. Therefore, your ego will say anything to prevent you from being mindful: you don't want to miss the next social media post, you have a show to watch, your to-do list has 17 items left on it, you're half an hour behind on your project, you'd better post on Facebook to get more likes…you get the idea.

Keeping your mind in that state of constant activity is a great way to get little to no work done—and to make mistakes on the work you DO accomplish. Mindfulness allows you to focus more, be more productive, and do your tasks right the first time. (And trust me, you won't actually miss most of the things you're afraid of missing out on.)

- **Mindfulness is boring!**

Many people have the perception that being mindful is not fun—after all, you're doing nothing! How is that exciting? But that perception isn't accurate. Mindfulness is not about being motionless and doing nothing. Mindfulness is about being present, aware, and curious for every second while doing the things you'd be doing anyway.

When you're having a conversation with your partner and feel upset, do you let those feelings control you, or do you observe them and ask what information they're giving you? When you're meeting with customers and you feel fear, do you tell yourself you're a timid person and can't do anything about it, or do you allow the fear to teach you how best to move forward? When you're working, exercising, traveling, or playing with your kids, are you on autopilot or are you aware of what's coming up for you from moment to moment?

Mindfulness is a challenging, stimulating activity that demands your full focus—and it can be practiced anytime, from sitting quietly at your desk to playing basketball to negotiating with your boss.

- **Don't I have to meditate all day to be mindful? I'm not a monk! Besides, stopping in the middle of a negotiation to find inner peace or whatever is too slow—I've got to react quickly, not stop to meditate.**

This is a common misconception around mindfulness: that it's the same as meditation. Yes, meditating can help with becoming more mindful, but you don't have to assume the lotus position, close your eyes, or chant "*Om*" to practice mindfulness. You don't have to meditate at all if you don't want to!

Being mindful doesn't mean shutting out everything else or retreating into some mental inner sanctum. Being mindful is simply paying attention to what emotions are coming up in a given moment. And while it does take a little more time than an unconscious reaction might, it's *not* stopping for five minutes in the middle of a meeting to close your eyes and breathe.

As limiting as they are, most of these excuses bring up a valid point: it's hard to embrace doing something you don't know how to do. And as we've talked about already, no one really teaches mindfulness in business or negotiation these days. So, it makes sense that many people (perhaps even you!) might see it as harder, slower, or more complex than it really is—even as they recognize how helpful it can be for them.

Fortunately, there's a system for creating mindfulness in your life that makes the process smooth, simple, and straightforward. This is what I've used with hundreds of clients over the last 20 years, and it allows them to separate from their egos, see their emotions from an observer's point of view, and get the kind of negotiation results I got in Japan. In the next chapter, I'll share my system with you.

Explorations

1. Focus on what your little voice is telling you after reading this chapter and be curious about it. Take a moment to feel which emotions are growing or already there.

Be curious: Why do you feel these emotions?

Where in your body do you feel them?

If you don't feel anything at all in your body, why do you think that is?

2. Remember the last time you were excited. Do you remember the occasion or the situation?

Reconnect with it.

What was the origin of this excitement?

What was happening with the rest of the world, your worries, etc.?

What was happening with time? Did you feel it went faster or slower?

3. Remember the last time you were angry. You were very likely not mindful. What can you learn from it?

Connect with the reason why you were angry.

Did you feel your anger was controlling you?

Were you aware that you were angry?

Are you afraid of your anger? What is the reason for your fear?

What would be the impact on your anger if you could name it from an observer's point of view?

Alexis confronts her fear

"Are you sure you can always choose other options?" Alexis asked when Mia *answered the phone three days later.*

"Yes, I'm sure," said Mia. *"And hello to you, too. Everything okay?"*

"Sorry, hi!" said Alexis. *"And…not exactly. I've been doing the exercise you gave me, and I've been getting better at being aware of what I'm feeling and when it's from my ego, but I'm hitting a block when I try to choose to feel something else."*

"Alright," said Mia. *"Tell me more about that."*

"Well…okay, so today I butted heads with Jorge a little bit. He wants me to be more aggressive and demanding, and I know that's just not who I am, but when I tried to tell him that, he bit my head off and told me to quit being so emotional…"

"…and you froze again?" finished Mia.

"Yeah, I did," admitted Alexis. "I knew it was my ego telling me to do that, and I thought of like four other things I could do, but I couldn't make myself choose them. It feels like my ego is always going to get out ahead of my mindfulness and trigger a feeling before I can stop it. Like when Lucas was shouting at me, that was like flipping a switch! Zero to paralysis in 3.2 seconds. And there wasn't anything I could do."

Mia nodded slowly. "I can understand that. And you're not the first person I've worked with who felt that way—not by a long shot. The solution to that particular problem—the problem of dealing with pre-set or deep-seated triggers—lies in the piece of the puzzle we haven't quite gotten to yet."

"Oh, good!" said Alexis, relief filling her voice. "I was hoping there was something else that could help me. What is it?"

"You already know the first step in this process of mindfulness is awareness of what you're feeling, and the second step is curiosity about why you're feeling it. And the final step is choosing to feel and act differently than your ego wants you to.

"But we skipped the third step in this mental process, which is what allows you to make that choice: compassion."

"Compassion?" Alexis echoed.

"Yes, Alexis, compassion. Specifically, compassion for yourself."

"I don't follow."

"Let me tell you a story, then," said Mia. "Early in my career, I was terrified to speak to the high-level executives in my company. My little voice kept saying things like, 'what if they don't have any time for me? What if they don't think I have anything valuable to say? What if I say the wrong thing? What if I make them angry?' All those ego messages ran around and around in my head all day long, and I couldn't get rid of them.

"So, of course, whenever I had to talk to one of the execs, to give a presentation or report on a project or even just talk about a next step, I got so stressed I could barely talk at all. It was like I couldn't even open my mouth until they left the room!"

Alexis' eyes were wide. "That couldn't have been good. How did you fix it?"

"My coach at the time asked me where that fear was really coming from. At first, I didn't get what he was asking—clearly, it came from what the execs could do to me if I screwed up, right?"

Alexis nodded.

"But my coach guided me to look deeper, past the fear of getting fired to a deeper fear of being judged or rejected, and finally past that to what was really going on: my ego made me deeply afraid of speaking to authority figures. And why was that? Because when I was a young girl, my mom taught me that it was never okay to challenge her authority.

"See, my mom was obsessed with the image of our family being perfect and high-achieving. We kids had to look like "good kids" all the time—clean and modest clothes, good grades, flawless manners, the works. And to do all of that, we had to do everything her way—and if we ever failed to do that or even questioned it, she flew off the handle.

"I remember once having an argument with her about whether I could do my homework after dinner instead of before dinner. It wasn't a huge deal. I'd have gotten it done either way. But my mother turned it into an excuse to scream at me for half an hour about how I never listen to her and how our family image would be ruined if I didn't do exactly as she said. I was 10 years old. And that kind of thing happened a couple of times a month at least. I finally just stopped talking to her."

"So, you were afraid to talk to the execs because in your mind—or rather, in your ego—they represented your mom, and talking to them triggered the fear of getting yelled at for challenging her authority?" asked Alexis.

"Exactly," said Mia. "That fear ran deep, deeper than anything I'd learned in school or in training. I couldn't logic my way out of that fear. I couldn't force my way past it. And I couldn't just ignore it. But I could use mindfulness to make myself more aware of it when it was happening. And that's what my coach taught me to do."

"Okay, that makes sense," said Alexis. "So, where does compassion come in?"

"Right there," said Mia. "I had to face that fear—and when I did, I had to meet it with compassion."

"What would that even look like?" Alexis wondered.

"I see compassion as a combination of understanding, acceptance, and empathy. So, the next time I had to meet with my boss's boss, I took some time the night before to understand, accept, and empathize with the fear my ego wanted me to surrender to. I actually had a conversation with myself, talking to my ego right there at my kitchen counter.

"First, I said, 'I understand why you're so scared of this. Mom trained you to be afraid of authority figures.' Then I said, 'I accept that this is a deep, natural fear and that you're going to want me to feel it every time I talk to an executive or another high-level authority figure.' And finally, I said, 'It's okay to feel this fear. It doesn't make you weak or childish or incompetent to be afraid. But it also doesn't mean I have to let your fear control me.'"

"And did that work?"

"Yes!" said Mia. "It wasn't 100% right away, and I definitely still felt scared for a long time after. But starting then, I was able to gradually speak more in executive meetings, and then speak more confidently, and eventually lead presentations."

"Are you still afraid of authority figures now?" asked Alexis.

"Yes, I am," said Mia with a sad smile. "I probably always will be, at least a little. But I've been able to use mindfulness to know when my ego wants to let that fear take over, and then meet it with compassion, so it doesn't feel like such a threat anymore."

Both women sat quietly for a moment, thinking. Then Alexis asked, "Does this mean my next assignment is to explore the deeper triggers behind why Lucas yelling at me was so scary?"

Mia nodded. "That's it exactly. Somewhere behind the scared woman in that meeting room is a frightened child or a rejected teenager, someone whose ego learned at a formative age to avoid getting yelled at. I want you to find that person, and I want you to show them the compassion they desperately need."

Alexis swallowed hard. "That sounds even tougher than reliving the meeting with Lucas."

"Yes, it does," said Mia. "Nevertheless, it's the next step in what I have to teach you. Will you do it?"

"Alright," said Alexis. "I'll do my best."

"Good," said Mia. "Now, this part of the process is something we'll do together, here on the phone. Are you ready?"

"As ready as I'm going to be, I think," said Alexis.

"First question, then. Why does it bother you so much when Lucas or Jorge yells at you?"

"Because I can't say anything back to them. Even when I feel like I could or should, nothing comes out."

"Why can't you say anything?"

"Because Jorge is my boss, I can't talk back to him. And Lucas could kill my career, so I can't argue with him, either."

"If you really wanted to badly enough, you could stand up for yourself—even with a boss or a powerful negotiation partner. Why don't you want to?"

"I do want to!" cried Alexis. "I have things to say! Smart things, helpful things! But I physically can't make myself say any of them. My body literally shuts down, and I can't open my mouth."

"Why does your body do that?"

"I have no idea!" Alexis wailed.

"I think you know more than you want to admit—even to yourself," said Mia gently. "Think about it and be curious. Why does your body respond like that?"

"Because of my ego?"

"Well, yes," said Mia wryly. "But why does your ego react so viscerally to aggressive men in authority getting upset with you?"

Alexis was quiet for a long moment.

"Alexis?" Mia asked softly.

"Because…because nobody wants to hear from a know-it-all girl." Alexis's voice was barely a whisper.

"And who told you that nobody wants to hear from a know-it-all girl, Alexis?"

An audible sniff. "My dad."

"Will you tell me more about that? Take your time," said Mia.

"My mom died when I was eight. My dad had three big, tough boys to play football with…and me, the little girl with her nose in a book. He used to like that I was smart—he and Mom would take turns reading to me. But after she was gone, it was like he couldn't even look at me. I think I reminded him of her too much."

"What did you do then?"

"I tried everything to get his attention. I'd crawl into his lap with a book to share, but he'd just turn up whatever game he and my brothers were watching on TV. I tried talking to him about things I'd learned that day, the way Mom used to, but *he tuned me out. After a few months of this, I started to get jaded, but deep down, I still wanted my daddy to love me like he used to, you know?" Alexis's voice broke on the last phrase, and Mia could hear her blow her nose.*

"You're doing fine, Alexis. When did your father tell you nobody wanted to hear from a know-it-all girl?"

"About six months after Mom died. It was spring, and he was trying to plan out all my brothers' summer sports games. I could tell it was taking him a long time, but I didn't know why—I only saw he was getting upset about it. So, I climbed up on the chair next to him to get a closer look."

"What did you see?"

"That he'd gotten two weeks mixed up. It was an easy mistake, with three different schedules and like five different sports to juggle. So I corrected him. I just took my little eight-year-old finger and pointed at the right week, and I said, 'It's this one, Daddy, not the one before.' And…and the next thing I knew, I was pressed up against the back of the chair, and my dad's face was right up close to mine, and he was yelling at me to shut up and leave him alone, no one wants to hear from a know-it-all girl." Alexis was crying openly now.

"What happened then?"

"I was eight! I started sobbing, of course," sniffled Alexis. "And my dad just said, 'Quit that whining, don't be a baby,' like he always said when any of my brothers cried, and turned back to the table."

"And how did you feel after that?" asked Mia.

Alexis blew her nose again. "I felt…like I'd done something wrong, and like I'd made my daddy hate me. But I also felt angry, because I hadn't done anything wrong! I'd only tried to help, and I'd gotten yelled at for it. I'd go back and forth between those two sides, actually. Sometimes I felt ashamed, and sometimes I felt angry, and sometimes I felt both at once, and whichever one I felt more I felt worse about not feeling the other one enough, and eventually, I just hated both of them so much I tried not to feel them at all."

"Can you see a connection between that whole mess of emotions and the situation you're dealing with now?" asked Mia.

"I think so," said Alexis, still crying softly. "When Lucas or Jorge yells at me, it puts me back in that chair next to my dad, torn between the shame of doing something wrong and the anger at getting yelled at for trying to help."

"Yes," said Mia quietly. "What else do you see?"

"Well…maybe that's why my body wants to freeze in response to the yelling? I'm feeling stuck between the two feelings—like if I do the wrong thing, I'll be in trouble, but if I do the right thing, I'll still get yelled at?"

"I think that's a very fair observation," said Mia.

"Thank you," said Alexis, wiping the last of her tears off her cheeks.

"How are you feeling now?" asked Mia.

"Wrung out and exhausted!" said Alexis. "I'm really glad I didn't have to go through it by myself, though. Thank you for talking me through it."

"You're welcome," said Mia. "You handled that much better than many people I've worked with. And now that we understand why your ego reacts to harshly to this particular situation, we can bring compassion to how it wants you to respond."

"Can you talk me through that part, too?"

"Of course! Tell me, how do you understand what happened now?"

"I understand that I didn't do anything wrong, that I didn't deserve my father's reaction, but that I've been living with the shame and anger of receiving it for years."

"And how do you accept it now?"

"I accept that this is a deep trigger for me, going back twenty years and that I'm probably going to feel those feelings whenever someone yells at me or gets aggressive with me, especially if it's a man who has more authority or seniority than I do."

"And how will you empathize with it going forward?"

"It's okay that my ego wants me to feel these emotions. It doesn't make me wrong or dumb or a failure just to feel them. But I don't have to let the feelings paralyze me. I do have the ability to look at them as separate from myself instead of just who I am."

"Very good, Alexis," said Mia. "How do you feel now?"

"Shaky," said Alexis. "I want to believe that fixed everything, but how can I know for sure? Until I get yelled at again, I mean?"

"Well, you can't really," said Mia gently, "but remember, this wasn't about fixing everything right now. It was about giving you the tools to get better as you practice *going forward. I won't sugar-coat it: you will feel those feelings again, many times. But now you have the key to letting them be only one option, an one option is that you can ignore or reject them."*

"And that's the next step of mindfulness? Choosing something other than what my ego is telling me I'm feeling?"

"Yes, and it's a courageous step. It takes a lot of bravery to stand up to your ego."

"Maybe that's the first thing I need to choose to stand up to, then," said Alexis.

"I like that plan," said Mia.

"Alright, what's next?"

"Tonight, nothing. Get a good night's sleep. Tomorrow we'll meet again and put everything together."

Chapter 4

THE KEY TO UNLOCK THE POWER OF MINDFULNESS

"Once we start basing our self-esteem purely on our performance, our greatest joys in life can start to seem like so much hard work, our pleasure morphing into pain."
—Kristin Neff

Being mindfully curious about your inner experience can bring up vulnerability, pain, fear, self-judgment, and shame. Whether it's the first time in your life that you've faced your emotions or if you've tried in the past, it's not an easy experience.

You might struggle to stay present and face your emotions. You might feel like no one else is dealing with these feelings—and thus, that you're not perfect or not as good as anyone else. You might even feel victimized by the feelings and want to reject them entirely. Any of those responses, while natural and valid, can derail your attempts to break past your ego.

So, as Alexis learned, simply being aware of your emotions and curious about why your ego is sending them to you isn't enough to be truly mindful—let alone to grow as a person or a be better negotiator.

Before you can access a different way of being, one that is not ego-driven, you need to unlock the gateway with self-compassion.

Merriam Webster defines compassion as "sympathetic consciousness of others' distress together with a desire to alleviate it." In other words, understanding and relating to the emotional pain other people are going through, without judging them for it. So, having compassion for yourself means understanding and relating to the emotional pain *you're* going through, without judging *yourself* for it.

If you feel vulnerable and pained by experiencing your emotions, self-compassion will help you stay present in the face of those emotions—even when your ego is screaming at you to run away.

For your ego, running away from your emotions is a great thing to do, as it leaves your ego in control of you. That's exactly what your ego wants—control allows it to hide from the pain it doesn't want to feel. However, that pain will come back later, as your ego will continue to be triggered by other situations life will present to you. You will be stuck in the same painful environment each time your ego gets triggered. Ultimately, the more you resist the pain of your emotions, the more acute they become.

As you learned in chapter two, your ego developed when you were a child. The emotions you experience today are most likely reactions to events that happened way back then when you were younger, and your ego was still forming. The events or situations are embedded deeply in your subconscious blueprint. So, today, when you face a tough situation or meet an emotional trigger, the primitive part of your brain relates it to your blueprint, which activates your ego and causes an emotional reaction.

You feel the pain rooted in these emotions because you've carried them inside you for a long time. But they don't belong to you. Compassion toward yourself will help you understand that it's time to accept those emotions for what they really are: a reaction today to events that happened long ago.

Self-compassion is the only way to eliminate your emotional pain for good, as it allows you to accept your emotions without letting them control you.

Now that you understand that the pain you feel today is coming from situations in your past, it's time to let go of that pain. Connecting with self-compassion also lets you have more compassion for your parents, teachers, classmates, or whoever hurt you. Whatever happened, they were acting without knowing that their ego was in control of them, because of situations that occurred when *they* were a child (and because they likely didn't even know they had an ego in the first place).

I know that what I'm sharing with you might be painful to acknowledge. It doesn't mean that you can't feel angry at people or situations from your past. However, to be free from them, you need to let the past go. It took some serious work on myself before I felt compassion for my parents, but growing compassion for myself ultimately helped me do it.

Another thing compassion will help you realize is that as a child, you were not responsible for what happened. You didn't create the situations that hurt you, and going through them was not your fault, whatever your ego wants you to believe and no matter what others might have told you.

Your ego wants you to believe that what happened in the past and the emotions you are experiencing today are happening **to** you, and it wants you to feel like a victim of your emotions. From an emotional and egoistic point of view, it is very tempting to believe that stuff happened in the past because you deserved it. From the same point of view, it's easy to believe that life is happening **to** you and no one else, that you are a victim.

It takes self-compassion to understand that you are not a victim, that life didn't happen *to* you—it simply happened. Self-compassion allows you to expand your perspective beyond what your ego wants you to believe about yourself, beyond the pain of your emotions. It gives you the option to accept and acknowledge the emotions without letting them victimize you. Compassion lets you tell your emotion: *I know you're there. I'm not your slave, and you can't control me.*

The more compassionate you are toward yourself, the less control your emotions have over you.

The bad news is, your ego knows this defense. When you can stay present with the pain of your emotions and use self-compassion to understand that they don't control you, your ego will quickly change gears and bring up self-judgment as a weapon.

Self-judging or auto-criticizing is one of the most powerful tools your ego has in its toolbox. Its job is to make you feel ashamed, deficient, and weak, especially compared to other people, just for having emotions in the first place. Even when you know that your co-workers or friends or negotiation opponents deal with ego and emotion too, your ego wants you to put them on the pedestal of perfection—and tear yourself down in the process.

Fortunately, self-compassion will help you to realize you are not alone in experiencing these emotions, and to remember that every human being has them every day. Self-compassion also reminds you that you are not flawed, deficient, stupid, or overly emotional, and that these painful emotions have nothing to do with your self-worth, regardless of what your little voice is telling you. Compassion helps you accept what you're feeling without judging yourself for feeling it.

Self-compassion creates distance between your emotions and you, which lets you experience them from an observer's point of view. This perspective lets you name what is happening while still being present and in control. When you can name it and be present, the pain will disappear soon after.

Back in my days as VP of global sales, after my Japanese negotiation story in the previous chapter, I was preparing with the executive team for a negotiation with a client in Thailand. While we were discussing different scenarios, my CEO abruptly said that he wanted me to increase the price by 17.5% (the most recent price increase for that customer had been three years prior and was less than 2%) and bring payment terms from 180 to 30 days (all customers in that region were paying at net 180 days). In my mind, there was no way this would work.

I acknowledged the fact that we were having a challenging year from a margin's perspective. Still, I felt the pressure of his demands, and I connected with my fears. I knew that he was wrong, but I felt paralyzed, and I was judging myself for not speaking up.

Mentally, the walls were closing in on me. Voices around me were muffled, the room seemed to darken, and I struggled to breathe. My boss (who reported directly to the CEO) was quiet and not even looking at me. I felt like my entire existence was threatened.

After what seemed like an eternity, but was really only a few seconds, I connected with compassion. I reminded myself that I wasn't wrong to feel fear or pressure around the CEO's demands, and that not wanting to speak up in the face of those emotions didn't make me a failure. In that moment, I felt the strength and courage to speak up fill my mind and body. I looked my CEO in the face and told him it was impossible to achieve everything he wanted me to accomplish in a single negotiation without damaging the relationship and risking losing the client.

I'd love to tell you that finding self-compassion that one time magically fixed the whole situation. Unfortunately, it wasn't that easy. The CEO exploded at me in response. He told me to "do my effing job," and if I was unable to do my effing job, that he had a pile of effing resumes on his desk, and he would find someone else to do my effing job! I never heard so many F-bombs in such a short time, let alone so many directed at me.

Fortunately, I was able to stay with self-compassion the rest of the day. Late that evening, I finally came to understand that it wasn't about me; it wasn't personal. My CEO must have been under a tremendous amount of pressure to deliver the promised earnings. The fact that I spoke up in front of everybody else must have triggered his ego.

Thirty hours of flights and connections later, I was in a suburb of Bangkok in a car with my local sales rep driving to meet our client. I shared with my rep that I'd been ordered to get the 17.5% price increase and net-30 schedule. The rep was as skeptical as I was, but understood that these numbers came directly from the CEO.

As expected, the client was very angry at me when I gave them the proposal. After two hours of negotiation, they brought their CEO in to leverage his seniority to have me back down from my position…and I couldn't. Because my numbers came from my CEO, I had no breathing room, no way even to say "okay, I'll go back and see what we can do."

During this meeting, self-compassion helped me to realize that it wasn't personal for these people, either. They weren't really angry at me; they were angry because their egos were in control. With this awareness, I was able told the client that I understood their frustrations and emotions, and unfortunately, there was nothing I could do. They said that I would regret it…but they ended up accepting the proposal.

Contrary to any other agreements I'd settled before, I didn't feel any joy or satisfaction. I didn't even think I'd proved myself to my CEO. I was exhausted. On my way back to the airport, I sent an email to my boss, telling him that the deal was done…but in my mind, I wondered how much longer this customer would actually stay with us.

It turned out I was right. The client postponed their first order by three months. When I picked up the phone and called them, they weren't forthcoming about the reasons for the delay. It felt like pulling teeth. When I pushed them to let me know when I could expect the order to be sent in, they told me that following my meeting with them, their board of directors decided to invest in a different technology my company wasn't involved with, which would be cheaper in the long term. By pushing unworkable numbers and leaving no room for flexibility, we'd ruined our working relationship with this client and lost the deal in the long run.

From where I sat with self-compassion, I completely understood. I'd have done the same thing in their shoes. I also understood that losing this deal wasn't something I needed to feel ashamed of, as my ego was clearly trying to tell me to do. None of it was personal. I'd done my job and things fell apart for reasons outside my control. I even was able to resist (barely!) the ego-driven impulse to tell my boss "I told you this would happen, and no one listened to me."

Anyone can be curious about what they are experiencing inside of them. That's not always familiar, but it's pretty easy. The challenge is to observe that experience without letting it control you or judging yourself for having it.

Connecting with self-compassion is the most demanding and gratifying action you can take. It's the most demanding because of the level of pain you'll face when doing it. It's the most rewarding because once you do it, your emotions will dissipate, and only then will you be able to realize that you have a choice of different behaviors that are not ego-driven.

Self-compassion is the most powerful tool you have to help you control the pain of your emotions, as it tells your primitive brain that it's okay, there is no danger, and you can face your emotions without running away from them. This will allow you to make the courageous choice to do something other than what your ego wants.

Explorations

Self-compassion allows you to stay present to your emotions without being under their control or judging yourself for feeling them. Understanding that your ego is the main reason preventing you from accessing self-compassion, let's be curious about the following questions:

1. What is your relationship with self-compassion?
2. Does it change with time or does it depend on the circumstances?
3. What emotions come up when you try to connect with self-compassion?
4. Where in your life have you struggled to find self-compassion?
   a. Are there events in your past that left you feeling guilty, ashamed, or angry with yourself?
   b. How do you think and feel about yourself today as a result of those events?
   c. Can you bring compassion to those memories? What happens when you do?
5. What will happen if you connect with self-compassion now?
   a. What are you afraid you will to lose?
   b. What can you potentially gain by *not* listening to your little voice?

Mia Puts It All Together

"Alright, Alexis," said Mia as they finished their coffee. "Walk me through what we've done so far."

"Um...well, first we went through my feelings during the meeting with Lucas. Then we talked about where those feelings came from, and why my ego wanted me to feel them. After that, we talked about how to choose different paths through mindfulness, and then last night, we added compassion as the key that allows me to make that choice. Oh, and we've also talked about how all this is something I need to practice, not just something to do once."

"Good summary!" said Mia. "Now tell me, how do you intend to practice all these different pieces of mindfulness?"

Alexis cocked her head, considering. "Actually...I'm not completely sure yet. I mean, I can try to do the kind of things you've talked me through over the last few days, and that feels like a start, but is that all there is to it? And I'm not sure I can do it all myself as easily as I did it with you, especially the compassion part."

"That's totally understandable. Separately, these steps can feel like a lot. But the good news is, they create a natural sequence that makes following them a lot easier—both in practice and in real situations."

Alexis nodded. "That makes sense. I feel like you kind of took me through part of that already, actually, just without saying that's what you were doing."

"That's because I did! I'm sneaky like that," laughed Mia. "The process of mindfulness has four steps. First, connection with yourself—notice what you're feeling in the moment. Second, curiosity—ask yourself why that feeling is coming up and what your ego is reacting to. Third, compassion—reassure yourself that it's okay to have those feelings, but that you aren't their victim. And finally, change—choosing to do something other than what your ego wants."

"Right," said Alexis slowly. "And now my job is to put the four together and practice them in that sequence?"

"Exactly," said Mia. "The four Cs for you to practice—I actually call it the 'C4U™' system."

"Nice! Okay, I can do that," replied Alexis. "But I'm still worried about a couple things."

"Such as?"

"Well…when I did these steps by myself, or you helped me do them, they took a long time. Multiple hours, sometimes days! How am I supposed to follow this C4U sequence in a meeting when I only have a few seconds to respond?"

"Great question. Remember when I told you that mindfulness is a skill, just like throwing a ball or playing an instrument?"

"Yes, and I get that I have to practice, but—"

"It's not just that you practice, it's how you practice," Mia said. "Practicing doesn't mean just repeating steps because I told you to. Practicing means internalizing how something feels. A skilled tennis player knows where the ball will go before they even finish their swing because they know what a good hit feels like. They don't have to think about it, they just know it, because they've done it so many times it's almost a reflex.

"And that's how mindfulness will become for you. Eventually, you will be able to connect with yourself, be curious, find compassion, and make a choice to change all within a few moments. So quickly that the people across the table from you might not even notice you've done anything."

"I will? Really?" Alexis was getting excited.

"If you practice the way I just described, yes. And it will happen sooner than you think. But for now, I don't want you to be in a hurry. I simply want you to practice the C4U sequence every hour or so until it starts to become second nature."

"Alright, I can do that," said Alexis. "The other thing I was worried about is—"

"Let me guess," said Mia. "How all this mindfulness stuff relates to negotiating?"

"Well, yeah. I get that keeping on top of my ego and not making emotional choices will help me stay calm when I'm talking to Jorge or Lucas, but I don't see how it actually makes me a more skilled negotiator."

Mia nodded. "It's not as big a gap as you might think. When you handle your ego, you get to choose to do something other than what it wants you to do. And negotiation is the art being able to pivot under stress and come up with second, third, and fourth options when it seems like you only have one. So, the two concepts have a similar foundation."

"Okay, that makes sense, but I still don't feel like I know how to come up with those options. Like, I could decide not to yell at Lucas when my ego wants me to, but *how do I know what kind of offer will work for him when the one Jorge told me to make doesn't?"*

"Ah, well, there we will need to get into some of the ins and outs of negotiation itself. But don't worry, I'll help you with that over the next few days. For now, all I want you to do is start internalizing this C4U™ system. Practice it in quiet moments where nothing's at stake, then gradually try some faster or more stressful situations and see how you do. And if you find yourself in another argument with Jorge, just let yourself remember the system and see if anything comes up. Okay?"

"Okay," said Alexis. "I'm still nervous about the Lucas meeting, but I guess that's still a week away, right? I'll be ready by then, won't I?"

"You certainly will," said Mia. "But for now, you've made some great strides already, so I'd like to introduce you to one more C."

"Wait, there's a fifth C?"

"Yes, and it's my favorite one. The fifth C stands for 'celebrate!' Every time you handle your ego and make a different choice, you've won a victory. And victories deserve a celebration! So, before we start getting into the negotiation side of this, we're going to brunch with Jonathan and the rest of your group, on me."

Alexis smiled. "I think I'm going to like this C, too!"

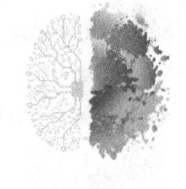

Chapter 5

THE C4U™ SYSTEM: FOUR STEPS TO MINDFULNESS

*"Instead of resisting any emotion, the best way to dispel it
is to enter it fully, embrace and see through your resistance."*
—Deepak Chopra

Remember, while being mindful is not that difficult, your ego doesn't like it when you are aware. Your ego is a construct from your past. Being mindful takes place in the current moment. Your ego is going to work hard to ruin that moment by bringing up difficulties from the past or raising concerns about the future. It will also make you ignore your body and find refuge in your head, where your little voice will try to tell you that "it is what it is," you don't have a choice or can't change.

To defeat your ego, you need a methodology or a system to help you relax in the current moment—without dwelling on the past or worrying about the future.

The four-pillar system Mia just described is a real process that will help you do exactly that. Here are the four steps you'll take to attain mindfulness in any moment:

C1: Connection. By connecting with yourself, you can mute the external world and clearly sense what is happening inside of you (emotions, tensions, feelings, etc.).

C2: Curiosity. Once you know what's coming up, you can be objectively curious about why it's there and what it means.

C3: Compassion. Compassion allows you to acknowledge the emotion without taking it personally, so you can accept the situation for what it is rather than what your ego wants you to think it is.

C4: Change. Instead of helplessly following your ego, now you can courageously choose to detach from it and do something different than it wants you to do.

In this chapter, we'll go through each of these pillars in detail.

C1: Connection with yourself

To connect with yourself, take a moment to block out external stimuli and focus your attention inward. This simple task is more challenging than it sounds, as your mind has been trained and coached to concentrate its attention outward to other people, external events, or objects.

This is where the "I don't have time" excuse comes up most often. But let me ask: if you feel you don't have time to stop and be mindful because you're too busy, too stressed, or your life feels out of control…where is that belief coming from?

That's right: your ego is the one telling you that. As counterintuitive as it may sound, the more you feel your life is out of control, the more you will benefit from slowing down for a minute. I'm reminded of a famous conversation with Mahatma Gandhi. When he announced an intention to meditate for one hour a day, one disciple said that the Mahatma's schedule was too full to allow that much time. Gandhi's response: "If I am that busy, then I must meditate for two hours a day instead of one." Don't fall into your ego's trap right off the bat here. As long as nothing is on fire (literally or figuratively), take the moment to connect.

Now once you're in the moment, what do you do with it? Just think about what's happening? Not exactly. Connecting with yourself is not simply thinking about what is going on. It's removing your focus from the external world and placing it on what is present inside of you. In particular, focusing on what's coming up in your body.

Why? Because we've all been conditioned to ignore our bodies and focus on our brains. But this system is about handling emotion, and we don't feel emotion in our brains. We feel emotion in our bodies. So, by connecting with what's present in our bodies, we get information that our heads can't give us.

After the China trip in chapter 1, when I stopped to connect with myself, this is how I felt: my body was very tense, my breathing was shallow, and the muscles in my neck were like a block of concrete. I was overwhelmed, angry, and felt powerless, and my body reflected those feelings. The only thing I wanted to do at that moment was to stop connecting with what was inside of me and keep things moving. But stopping and focusing on myself brought me new information I wasn't aware of.

Contrast that with how I felt during the negotiation in Japan in Chapter 3. I was very grounded and calm, my breathing was deep and slow. My senses heightened, making me aware of the entire environment (even noticing a slight wind draft moving the curtains in the room). It was as if time slowed down drastically. I felt Zen.

This is what connecting with yourself looks like. It doesn't take a lot of time, but it does take the willingness to slow down and listen to your body in the moment.

C2: Curiosity about what is going on internally

Now that the world has slowed down and your focus is inward, the priority is to be curious about what you've noticed and felt coming up.

Being curious is not the same as solving a problem. You don't have to reach an endpoint, find a solution, or take action. This is not the time to fix anything. The intent here is to observe what is going on and be curious about it from a detached position. Avoid the temptation to judge what you see (right or wrong) or blame anyone (yourself, others, or the situation) for it.

Instead, ask yourself open-ended questions about what you see and feel coming up in your body, and then listen carefully to the answers. Sometimes, you'll even ask the same question over and over again until you get an answer that feels genuine. The essential element is not to try to guess or predict what the answers will be, nor to grab at the most obvious or familiar ones. Curiosity isn't *thinking* so much as *feeling*. Feel what is going on your body as you ask the questions below, and let those feelings guide you.

Here's what that typically looks like:

First, start your observation with one of the following prompts:

- I'm observing…
- I'm seeing…
- I'm realizing…
- I'm noticing…
- I'm experiencing…

And complete the statement with an emotion or feeling in your body, such as:

That…

- I'm angry
- I'm frustrated
- I'm judging myself or others
- I'm scared
- I feel like a victim
- I want to punch something
- My little voice is really loud
- I'm feeling lost and confused
- I want to start crying
- I feel the urge to run away

(You may notice that these first two steps overlap very closely with the connection to yourself you began in C1. That's not a coincidence! As you get more comfortable with this system, the C1 and C2 steps will start to happen almost simultaneously.)

Then, start asking yourself open-ended questions about those emotions:

- Why do I feel this emotion right now?
- Where is it coming up in my body?
- What specifically triggered this feeling?
- When was the last time I felt it?
- What am I afraid of/angry at/sad about?
- What's happening that isn't meeting my needs or expectations?
- Why are those needs and expectations so important?
- What do I really want here?
- Why do I want it so badly?

As you receive each answer, consider it, and then ask another question. Follow the chain of answers until you feel you've reached the real foundation of what's coming up for you.

Fair warning: This will not be easy at first, for two reasons.

First, because the minute you start to be curious, you will confront difficult emotions—anger, fear, frustration, guilt, and so on. Which means you'll be face to face with your ego. And your ego doesn't like being confronted! It prefers to stay hidden in the lower levels of your brain—where it can easily disguise itself as you. So, when you start to look deeper than your ego's surface-level messages (your emotions) and ask *why* you're feeling them, the ego wants to fight back. Usually, it does this by reacting to the first difficult emotion you encounter with a simple message: "Stop that!"

The way you feel when those tough emotions are present remind your ego of feeling threatened. So, its immediate response is to protect itself by telling you to stop being curious! This may come up as feelings of fear, anxiety, or shame. It may feel like a sense of futility—like this is just the way things are, and there's nothing you can do to change them. It may appear as a desire to blame someone else or make excuses for yourself. It can even come up as a sense of just being done—that just discovering this first level of feeling is enough, you don't need to go any deeper, everything's fine, nothing to see here.

All of these feelings and thoughts are distractions set up by your ego to make you *stop looking*. And because they paint curiosity as an uncomfortable activity, it's easy for these messengers of ego to convince you to be curious for just a couple of seconds and then go right back to your fast-paced life.

Don't fall into this trap. Curiosity only works when you follow the questions all the way to their roots. Stopping after a few moments might bring short-term comfort, as it lets you avoid or ignore some tough emotions, but in reality, you just put a bandage on a wound that needs surgery.

Why? Because of the second reason curiosity isn't easy: it brings up deep-seated issues from your past.

The deeper your questions go into the "why" of what's coming up for you, the more likely they are to lead to memories of painful or traumatic past events, particularly from your formative years. These events are what your reptilian and mammalian brains draw on when evaluating threats; they happened while those parts of your brain were fully evolved, but your frontal lobe was still developing (i.e., when you were a child).

These discoveries can trigger stronger, more primal emotions like rage, grief, self-judgment, sadness, and pain. These emotions live in the deep part of yourself that you don't spend a lot of time in. They're unfamiliar and frightening—so much so that you may have blocked them out. Just getting in touch with them can feel completely overwhelming. You may want to stop right there and give up—or even run away as fast as you can.

The problem is, mindfulness lives on the other side of this level of understanding. If you stop being curious you won't be able to understand the meaning of what is happening inside of you. Instead, you'll be right back under the control of your ego, who would always rather you react from emotion than be mindful. However, if you continue with curiosity from an observer's point of view, you will realize that facing past difficulties is only the beginning, not the end of the experience. The only way out is through.

The good news is that by purposefully being an observer and naming what is happening, you remove much of the threat and detach the experience of curiosity from the emotion it explores. Naming an emotion and asking questions about it triggers the frontal lobe rather than the lower levels of the brain—conscious thought, not instinctive reaction. This allows you to remember that you are not the emotions you're experiencing—if you were, you couldn't observe or be curious about them.

Being an observer helps you realize that you are not what you are sensing—otherwise, you wouldn't be able to observe it.

But even knowing that, facing difficult moments and painful memories from your past is really, really hard. Curiosity alone is rarely enough to bring you through it. The only way to stay with what is coming up is not only to be curious but also to have compassion for yourself.

C3: Compassion toward yourself

Asking yourself questions and being curious about your inner experience can bring up vulnerability, pain, fear, anger, self-judgment, or shame. Staying present to all these emotions and feelings can be overwhelming. This is normal! No one can confront themselves this deeply and just brush it off. Whatever you may be feeling right now, there's nothing wrong with feeling it.

Knowing this is the first step in having compassion for yourself.

Self-compassion is being gentle and supportive with yourself, understanding that whatever comes up is not right or wrong. It just is. Nobody can challenge the way you feel in the moment. There's no shame or guilt or failure in feeling the way you do. Self-compassion also continues your role of observer, where you see the emotions and difficult memories as separate from yourself. These things don't threaten you or trigger your ego because all you're doing is observing them.

To do this, name what is actually happening in your deepest moments of curiosity:

- I'm judging myself for…
- I'm ashamed of…
- I'm criticizing myself because…

When you name what you are experiencing, you are not the experience anymore. You just became an observer. You are not the emotion you feel because you are just watching what is going on. If you were the emotion, you wouldn't be able to see it.

You Are Not What is Coming Up.

Again, though, this isn't always as easy as it sounds. Your ego doesn't like this step at all! In fact, it's probably in fight-or-flight mode by now and wants to get you out of there as soon as possible. Your ego doesn't want you to be compassionate for yourself, because doing so breaks its control over you even further. It will fight hard to annihilate your self-compassion. Don't feel bad if you struggle with it.

In time, you will get better at expressing compassion for yourself. But when you're first learning how, I recommend reaching out to someone you trust for help. If you are already working with a therapist, personal development group, coach, or counselor, talk to them. If you feel comfortable sharing these feelings and memories with a close friend or family member, do that.

The intent in reaching out is to get support in muting your little voice by getting someone else to help you see it isn't you. That person can hold up a mirror in front of you that doesn't reflect your ego, self-judgment, or self-criticism. All it reflects is the truth of what is coming up for you, and kindness and forgiveness toward yourself for feeling it. In time, you'll be able to hold this mirror up for yourself, but having outside support (like Mia provided for Alexis) will be invaluable early on.

As you embrace compassion and observe the situation through its lens, you start to experience a new perspective—one fully detached from emotion. From that observing point of view, there are no expectations, no desires, no fears, no comparisons or drama, just observing from an emotional distance without judging or criticizing. Time slows down, and you are fully aware of the moment. It feels like a new reality, where for once your ego is silent. You can listen to your true self, your intuition, and choose to act without the control of emotion or instinct. This is how I felt in that meeting in Japan, and it's how you will learn to feel, too.

Once you reach this moment, you can connect with options and choices your ego is hiding from you. When you think you are what's coming up, you're too close to the emotion to react in any way except how your ego is telling you to. But when you become a compassionate observer, you distance yourself from the emotion—which lets you see and consider other options your ego doesn't want you to see. In other words, compassion allows you to change. *You can choose to do something different in the moment.*

C4: Change

When your ego is leading you, it often feels like you have no choice, like you're locked into doing what it tells you. From that perspective, it seems that you are going through life with the same thoughts, emotions, and situations repeating themselves. This is a big reason most people's lives seem to follow recognizable patterns of behavior over time.

The reality is you *do* have a choice. Remember, your ego is not who you are, it's a learned personality that doesn't control you unless you let it. You can choose not to do what your ego wants you to do, to behave not from your learned personality but from the real you. And once you've completed the first three steps of the C4U™ system, you're ready to make that choice.

How do we know how to choose something different than our ego wants? Or what else we can choose to do?

Start by asking yourself a new set of questions about your emotional situation. For example:

- What if there was another way of being?
- Who said I can't change?

- What if I didn't need anybody else to validate myself?
- What if I can behave in a way that it isn't driven by fear, a desire to please, or a desire to prove myself?
- What could I do if I didn't follow my ego right now?
- What options do I have that these emotions might be preventing me from seeing?

As you answer these questions for yourself and ask follow-ups if needed, new options and opportunities will start to show up as if a veil has been lifted. Some of them will be good, some might not be ideal, but no matter what you get to choose from them. Your ego doesn't get a vote anymore.

Making this choice to change isn't just the objective of the C4 step, it's also the beginning of a new neurological pathway within your brain. The more you do it, the easier it will become—your frontal lobe will literally rewire itself, directing more neurons toward slow, mindful, conscious thought and fewer toward the fight-or-flight instinct of your ego.

As you can imagine, this step is the biggest threat for your ego, so you might start hearing your little voice telling you that you don't really have this choice—or that it's the wrong choice to make. You might be scared of the unknown. You might worry that people won't appreciate you. You might be worried about not being "happy" anymore. And you'll almost certainly worry that changing your approach to a negotiation in the middle of a meeting might lead to catastrophe. Whatever your little voice is telling you, don't believe it. It is fake. Your ego doesn't want you to change. But change is what will allow you to break your ego's control.

Courage is making the choice to confront pain, danger, uncertainty, or intimidation despite your fear. You need courage to separate yourself from your ego and connect to your intuition, the place of knowing where you can act rather than react, because it won't be comfortable, and it may be scary. But once you find that courage to change, you will never look back.

C5: Celebrate!

"Wait. You mentioned 4Cs to change, but now there's a fifth one?"

That's right! When you finish going through the C4U™ system, you'll have just been through something very uncomfortable, painful, and scary…*and you're still here.* You didn't let your ego or your fear control you. You know things about yourself now you didn't know before. And you made a courageous choice to change how you responded to your situation—responding based on your intuition, not emotion.

That's a really big achievement! Especially if you've never done it before! You should be proud and excited about it. Take a moment to recognize yourself and the growth you went through. Celebrate your happiness and freedom in this moment!

You might hear your little voice telling you that you haven't accomplished anything. But that's BS! Your ego only wants to celebrate on its terms—when you do something that makes *it* feel good. Usually, that's when you reach some arbitrary milestone…and then after you celebrate for all of ten seconds, your ego is already moving the goalposts and wanting even more. So, don't listen to the idea that you didn't accomplish anything worthwhile by putting this system into practice. It's not really you, and now you know it isn't!

As a way to anchor this moment of celebration, I encourage you to share your mindful experience with someone you trust and invite them to celebrate with you. You also may want to journal about your experience, whether you share it with anyone or not, so you'll always remember what happened and how it felt.

Connect with yourself and become an observer of your own experience. Don't be afraid of being curious and explore where it is taking you. Bring compassion toward yourself when you start judging and comparing yourself, feel ashamed, or scared. Then be courageous to listen and trust that your intuition or the feeling of knowing is the signpost you were looking for. Finally, celebrate your triumph over your ego! This is the C4U™ (C5U?) system.

In the rest of the book, we'll look closer at how to apply this system to negotiation, alongside skills and tactics that will set you up for success. This two-sided approach of skills and mindfulness is what I teach my clients, and what has allowed hundreds of them to find real, consistent, reliable negotiation success.

Explorations

One of the best ways to practice the C4U™ method is to bring it to a recent stressful or emotional moment and use it to explore that situation in hindsight. The following questions will help you do that. You don't have to answer all of them, but I strongly encourage you to go through the entire sequence of connection, curiosity, compassion, change, and celebration around the situation you have in mind. I also suggest writing down what comes up so you can refer to it later.

First, think of a situation you went through recently that brought up a lot of stress or emotion for you. It may be a negotiation, but it doesn't have to be! Place yourself back in that moment in your mind and take a few minutes to go through each of the C4U™ steps as if you were there right now.

C1: Connection with yourself: **Mute the stimulus from the external world.**

Take a moment to connect with what is coming up by remembering the emotions and feelings that came up for you then. Slow down and focus on how you felt in your body and your mind.

C2: Curiosity: **Become an observer of your own experience and name what is going on.**

Ask yourself these questions:

- Why do I feel this way?
- Where in my body do I feel...?
- What is my little voice telling me?
- What specifically triggered this feeling?
- What's happening that isn't meeting my needs or expectations?
- Why are those needs and expectations so important?
- What is distracting me from being mindful?

C3 Compassion: **Nobody can judge or exactly know what you feel inside of you.**

- Does my little voice get louder?
- Where is my comparative or critical judgment coming from?
- What am I learning here?
- What about this makes me feel threatened?
- Is it possible that I might be in the wrong? How does that make me feel?
- What am I facing in myself I might not have encountered before?

C4 Change: **There is another way. Connect with your intuition and make the courageous choice.**

- What is my little voice telling me that I would lose if I did something different?
- Is that true what my little voice is telling me?
- What if it's not true?
- Is it possible to let go of that directive?
- What could I do instead?
- What would happen if I did that?
- What would it take to make the choice to do it? What fear do I need to face?
- What is preventing me from asking for help?
- Who said if I asked for help, it meant that I'm not good enough or competent enough?
- What if my desire to change was stronger than my fear?

C5 Celebrate: **Be proud of yourself for what you have been through!**

- How do I feel now that I made a choice to change?
- Why was that the right choice for me?
- What am I doing differently now, and how am I thinking differently about it?
- What did I overcome by going through this process?
- What feels more powerful, happier, or more right for me about this path?

- What will I do differently the next time I face this issue?
- How is my relationship with my ego different now?
- Who can I share this moment of triumph with?
- What will I do to celebrate (by myself and with them)?

PART TWO

THE NEGOTIATION

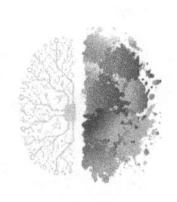

ALEXIS STARTS AT THE BEGINNING

I could really get used to this, *Alexis thought.*

She was sitting on Mia's porch again. The sun was sinking behind the trees around Mia's yard, and the remains of Thai takeout were scattered across the patio table. For a few moments, Alexis could forget about Lucas, Jorge, and the whole big ball of stress.

Mia came back with refilled wine glasses. "Ready to get started?"

Alexis heaved a sigh. "Yes…and no. I kind of just want to watch the sunset forever."

Mia laughed. "I know that feeling well. It's my favorite thing to do on this porch. But your meeting is in five days, and we've got to get you ready for it."

"I know, I know," Alexis grumbled. "Alright, let's get this over with. Here's what I'm supposed to offer Lucas this next meeting. How do I use C4U™ to get him to take it?" She pulled a folder out of her messenger bag and held it out to Mia.

Mia didn't take it. Instead, she sipped her wine, then said, "Alexis, do you remember when I asked you what you thought the point of negotiation was?"

Alexis blinked. "Yes, I think so. Why?"

"Because getting Lucas to accept the offer in that folder is not the point of negotiation. And as long as you think it is, C4U™ won't help you."

"Well, you didn't tell me what the point was when you asked me that!" Alexis said, a bit defensively. "You just said we'd talk about it later!"

"You're right," said Mia. "And it's later now. So, let's start there. Why do you think the point is to make Lucas accept the offer Jorge told you to make?"

"Because that's the best deal for us. It gets us the most money from Lucas and his company while giving them the least from our end."

"Okay, that seems logical enough. But how do you know that's the best deal?"

"Um…because we get the most and give up the least? Didn't I just say that?"

"Think deeper," said Mia. "How do you know the deal that gets you the most and gives up the least is the best deal for both parties? What if it isn't? What if there's a better deal you could come up with?"

"How could there be?" asked Alexis. "That doesn't make sense. Jorge is always saying the best deal is the one that gets the most while giving away the least, and our job is to make that happen any way we can."

Mia arched an eyebrow. "And you agree with Jorge on all of that?"

Alexis fidgeted. "Well…no, not exactly, but what else can I do? If I come back with a result that gets less or gives away more, I'll get in trouble and maybe lose my spot in the leadership development program."

"You want to maintain your relationship with Lucas and his company, don't you?" asked Mia.

"Absolutely," Alexis replied, not knowing why Mia was asking this question. "I can't afford to lose their business."

"Okay, how do you think Jorge will react if Lucas is upset and walks away because it's the best deal for you and not for them?" insisted Mia.

Alexis stared blankly at Mia. "I don't get it. Isn't the best deal for them the best one we offer? Don't they have to accept it, since they won't get a better one somewhere else? The fact that we get more out of the deal than them is just part of how it all works, right?"

"Not necessarily. Now listen carefully, Alexis. The point of negotiation is not to beat the other person, to get more from them than you give up, or even to find a compromise where at least both of you are unhappy. That's zero-sum negotiation, where for me to win, you have to lose. That's how negotiation has been taught for decades, and it's clearly Jorge's bread and butter, but it really doesn't work anymore—if it ever did."

Alexis frowned. "It doesn't? It seems to work for Jorge and everyone else he's taught."

"I don't know Jorge personally," mused Mia, "but if I had to guess, he's a one-trick pony. Intimidation and domination are all he knows how to do—and when you only do one thing, you can get pretty good at that thing. So, I'm not surprised he's had some success.

"But here's the thing about people like him. They're in their ego **all the time**. That makes it impossible for them to be flexible or even see that other options exist. If he ever meets someone who doesn't let him bully them, he's going to be out of luck. And guess what—there are a lot more people these days who don't like bullies at the negotiating table. That methodology is on its way out."

"Okay, I guess that makes sense," said Alexis. "I certainly don't want to be a bully! And I don't like that Jorge is one either—especially to me, but in general, too. But how do I approach negotiation instead? What will actually work for me here?"

"Let me answer that question with a question," replied Mia. "What does Lucas want out of this negotiation?"

Alexis looked up from her folder, surprised. "Um…I don't know. He didn't really tell me; he just said to go back and sharpen my pencil. Why?"

"Don't you think that if you gave him something he wanted, he'd be more likely to give you something you want?"

"I guess so," said Alexis. "And that doesn't mean that I have to give him something I don't want to give up?"

"Not necessarily," said Mia. "If he wants something you don't want to give, you can offer him something you're more comfortable giving instead, or ask for something more valuable in return, or get creative and find another option. The point is that when you negotiate with Lucas, the goal is to find a solution where both of you get the value you're looking for, not just you or him. Make sense?"

"I think so. It sounds like you're telling me to add value to the negotiation, not try to extract it."

"Right!" exclaimed Mia. "And that's a great way to put it, too—you're the first I've worked with to use those terms that way. Nice job."

Alexis grinned. "Okay, so how do I do that?"

"First of all, you embrace the idea you just put into words, that your only goal is to create as much value as possible for everyone involved—even if that means getting less money than you may have initially wanted."

"Okay, I know Jorge isn't going to like the less money part!" said Alexis, still grinning.

"Not even a little bit," laughed Mia. "But that leads to the second part: to realize that value doesn't always mean money. Sometimes value takes the form of time, or flexibility, or saving face, or a stronger relationship, or one of a dozen other factors that you or your counterpart might find valuable."

"I could see that" said Alexis. "When I was in that meeting with Lucas, I'd have gotten lots of value out of him just not yelling at me!"

"That's an ego example, but yes," said Mia. "Having a more friendly and supportive working relationship with Lucas and his company is one way you could get value that isn't money. Now, the next piece to keep in mind is that in order to create value for both sides, you need to know both sides—theirs and yours. That means being absolutely clear on what you need and taking the time to understand what they need—which is the opposite of Jorge's take-it-or-else strategy. Make sense?"

Alexis nodded, taking notes on the back of Jorge's folder.

"The final step is to understand that all of this takes time. Time to prepare, for one thing, and time to have multiple meetings with the other side—as well as time to reflect on those meetings and bring more value to the next ones."

Alexis frowned. "Multiple meetings? As in, more than like one or two? But what if we need a contract renewed right away? Jorge sent me to get the new contract from Lucas right now, not weeks or months from now."

"As many meetings as it takes to reach maximum value for both sides," Mia said. "Sometimes that can happen in just one or two meetings, but that's rare. Trust me, no matter what Jorge says, negotiations usually take time. The goal of each meeting is to get you to the next one with a little more information and a little more momentum until you reach the point where you created enough value for both of you to close the deal."

Alexis looked doubtful. "I don't think Jorge will like that much, but I guess I could try it."

"Good," said Mia. "Then we'll get started on the first part of a successful nego-tiation: preparation."

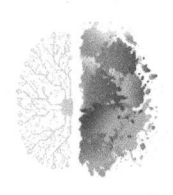

INTRODUCTION TO PART TWO

The first part of this book was all about understanding the problem and learning about the solution. That's great, but it can feel a bit abstract. How do you go from knowing about your ego and understanding the basics of the C4U™ system to applying and using that knowledge in stressful negotiation situations where your ego might be triggered?

That's what the second part of this book is here to help with. We'll keep following Alexis through her negotiation journey. As we do, we'll explore how learning and practicing the C4U™ system will make you a more successful negotiator.

The first thing to understand is the fact that negotiation is a process, not an event. There's a common misconception that "a negotiation" literally means one meeting, nothing before or after. This misconception has led to many companies pushing their people to close deals in a single session, as well as many negotiators focusing on the meeting itself and ignoring what happens (and what needs to happen) before and after it. So, when you try to learn negotiation, it's easy to focus all your attention on that one meeting and the specific skills you need in that high-pressure, high-stakes environment.

In reality, the negotiation process rarely concludes in a single meeting, nor does it only involve the meeting itself. Going through the negotiation process takes time and pushing or trying to complete it in one session is very likely going to derail the whole process and negatively impact the outcome. And a big reason for that is simply that when you're in a hurry, mindfulness tends to go out the window.

The second element is to understand this controversial but straightforward concept: the goal of negotiating is not to "win" or "beat the other person." When your ego is in control, it's all about you; you want to win, and you might not care if your win comes at a loss for or at the expense of the other side. Since almost all negotiations are ego-driven, the win-lose mentality is still commonly used by many people.

However (and thankfully!), most experts and trainers today are moving away from "winning" as a goal. While it can seem convincing and beneficial in the short term, it can be disastrous in the long run, as it doesn't create value for both sides. Trying to beat or defeat the person across the table from you not only triggers a lot of ego in both of you, but it also sets a terrible precedent for future meetings with that person. Do you think they'll be looking forward to negotiating with you again next month when ago you just tried to dominate and bulldoze them?

Similarly, negotiation isn't about meeting in the middle, splitting the difference, or finding a compromise where no one's happy. These approaches don't create value, they limit and sometimes eliminate value, and they lead to situations where one party has to lose for the other one to win. This approach may be calmer and more polite than the "beat the other person" approach, but it doesn't lead to any more success for each party.

The Real Goal of Negotiating is *to Create Value for Both Parties.*

Value creation is about expanding the pie and being creative with the solution. It's about understanding the other person's real concerns, challenges, and pain points and creating a mutually agreeable solution. You can't create value for anyone if you don't have a clear understanding of their motivations and what is going on in their world. You can't create value for the other person if your ego is in control. Creating value can only be accomplished by being mindful.

The second part of the book outlines the phases of negotiation like different parts of climbing a mountain. In each of these chapters, we will look at negotiation situations where your ego might be triggered. For each situation, we will show

how to leverage the C4U™ system to keep your ego in check and choose (or create) better options than it wants to offer you.

We'll also follow Alexis through her negotiation with Lucas, as she learns to put the C4U™ system to work in every moment of the process, from preparing for her next meeting to getting both of their bosses' signatures on the dotted line.

By the end of this section, you'll be ready to bring C4U™ to your next negotiation with confidence.

Chapter 6

THINKING AHEAD: HOW TO PREPARE MINDFULLY

"By failing to prepare, you are preparing to fail."
—**Benjamin Franklin**

Alexis Prepares—and Meets Her Ego

"Preparation?" asked Alexis. "The meeting with Lucas is in five days! And there's a leadership development program meeting the day before that where I'm supposed to tell everyone my plan for the Lucas meeting. I don't have time for a bunch of research, I've got to get ready!"

Mia gave a wry smile. "You do realize you just said you don't have time to get ready because you have to get ready, don't you?"

Alexis groaned. "Ugh, you know what I mean! I'm seriously freaking out here, will five days be enough to get C4U™ under my belt?"

"I don't know, will it?" asked Mia. "Let's find out. Now, let's go back to your first meeting with Lucas for another minute. Tell me, what was the objective of that meeting?"

"To get Lucas to renew the contract or pay list price."

"*Because his company had been paying discount price and delaying renewing the contract for several months, right?*"

"*Yes, exactly,*" said Alexis.

"*So, to put it another way, your job in that meeting was to deliver bad news to Lucas. Would you say that's fair?*"

"*I guess so.*"

"*And did you think you could do that?*"

"*I thought I could, sure,*" said Alexis. "*I mean, I wasn't completely confident, but Jorge had told me what to say, so I just said it.*"

"*I see. And did you think at all about what Lucas might have needed from you? Why coming to the meeting was important to him?*"

Alexis looked sheepish. "*No, it really didn't occur to me. I'm guessing it should have?*"

"*Probably, but we'll come back to that,*" said Mia. "*Between you and Lucas, or your company and his, who needs the other one more?*"

Alexis blinked. "*Um...I have no idea. Why does that matter?*"

Mia appeared to ignore the question. "*And I'm guessing you didn't prepare any further for that meeting? You didn't write out any questions to ask Lucas, or make any contingency plans in case he didn't respond the way Jorge said he would, anything like that?*"

"*No, I guess I didn't,*" said Alexis.

"*Understandable,*" said Mia. "*One more question: can you see how not preparing ahead of time created some problems for you in that meeting?*"

Alexis sighed. "*Yes, I can. But how can I figure out all the stuff you just talked about in just a few days? It sounds like way too much!*"

Mia held Alexis's gaze. "*It may feel like a lot now, but trust me, it's necessary—and it will help you. Now, I want you to go into C4U™ right now. What are you feeling at this moment?*"

Alexis bit back a sharp reply, took several deep breaths and closed her eyes. After a few moments, she said, "*I'm feeling panicked. You just told me that this is going to take a lot of time, and I don't have much.*"

"*What else?*"

"Um…I'm scared of Lucas, of course! I really don't want him to yell at me again! I'm afraid whatever I try with him isn't going to work, and he'll just start shouting, and I'll lose the contract and the opportunity of the leadership development program and my job and…yeah. Definitely feeling scared. I almost wonder if it's even worth preparing if he's just going to lay into me no matter what."

"Okay, good awareness. Now move into curiosity. Panic, fear, despair…why are these feelings coming up? What is your ego trying to do by bringing them to you?"

Alexis thought for several more moments. "I think it's trying to protect me."

"Protect you from what?"

"From being yelled at, from being humiliated, and from putting myself in a really stressful situation," listed Alexis.

"And what does your ego want you to do?"

"Not spend time preparing. Just accept that this is a loss, write it off, and wait until the next one when I have more time and a nicer person to negotiate with. Don't try to salvage this one, I'll only get hurt."

"How will you bring compassion to this moment?" asked Mia.

Alexis sat up a bit straighter and squared her shoulders. "Well, I totally get my ego wanting to protect me from getting yelled at by a man in authority. We talked about that the other day—it reminds me of my dad. So, maybe I'll start by saying that I know my dad loved me and that his reaction wasn't personal. He was just sad and struggling and didn't know how to be both a dad and a mom. So, as much as I appreciate my ego wanting to protect me from remembering that day, I don't need that protection anymore."

"Okay, then what?"

"Then…hmmmm. I think what comes next is to say that it's natural for me to feel anxious and scared right now, even panicked. It's true that I don't have a lot of time, and that I'm using that time to learn something totally new, and that I really don't know what I'm doing yet. It's totally logical that I'd be scared, right?"

"I'd agree with that," said Mia. "What else?"

"Well, that it's okay for me to feel fear right now, even to want to panic…but that I don't have to decide what to do now from that fear. I can acknowledge the fear, but it doesn't have to control me."

"Good!" said Mia. "That's three C's, now tell me what you'll do for the fourth. What will you do that's opposite of what your ego wants you to do?"

Alexis opened her eyes. "Um...take the time to prepare, I guess," she said a bit ruefully. "But I'm not sure what to prepare for, or how to do it, let alone when to fit it into the next few days. Will you help me with that?"

"Of course," said Mia. "That's what I'm here for. Now, let's start by talking about power..."

Would you climb Mount Everest without training, preparation, and planning?

On some level, we all know that we need to prepare for something as big as climbing a mountain or as vital as a negotiation. But every year, people die on mountainsides because they weren't adequately prepared. And every day, people fail at negotiating because they didn't get themselves ready to perform successfully.

Let's look at different situations during the preparation that could trigger your ego. Let's start by exploring situations where you are reflecting about yourself.

When You Have no Time to Prepare

Feeling unprepared, either for a negotiation meeting as a whole or in a particular moment of negotiating, is one of the biggest triggers for your ego to want to protect itself. Why don't you prepare (or prepare enough) for negotiations that will shape the future of your career?

One reason is thinking you have no time. Yes, preparing for a negotiation takes time away from other work, but it only takes a few failed negotiations to realize that preparation is worth prioritizing. Choose to prioritize preparation and see it as part of your overall job, even when it takes more time than you'd like.

A second reason might be that you think you know how to negotiate already, so you think you can rely on that knowledge in lieu of preparing. This reason can also come up when you're negotiating with a long-term customer—you've already negotiated with them for several years, so why would you need to prepare this time? But as we learned in the first half of this book, having negotiation skills isn't the same as being a successful negotiator—and even if you've negotiated with this customer many times, new emotions could still come up.

Let's be Honest Here: The Real Reason You Don't Prepare is Because of Your Ego.

Your ego doesn't want to admit that it doesn't know everything, doesn't control everything, and doesn't perform well under emotional pressure. Admitting those things feels threatening to your ego. This is why it comes up with excuses like the ones I just listed—even when you *know* that preparing will set you up for success, and even when past negotiations may have gone badly for you *because* you weren't prepared. Your ego deliberately makes you forget about prior negotiations where you felt emotional, wanted to give in, and/or were afraid of upsetting the other person because you didn't prep ahead of time.

Not being prepared will hinder your ability to negotiate successfully, because inevitably something will come up you aren't ready for. Suddenly you have to improvise under stress—likely with your ego and emotions trying to take over. Before you know it, you're reacting, defensive, and unable to see clearly.

Let's use the C4U™ system to learn more about why you don't prepare—and how you can choose a different option.

Let's pause for a moment (C1) and be curious (C2). Don't stop at the first answer you are discovering; keep asking why.

1. What is preventing you from taking the time to prepare?
2. What are you afraid of about preparing?
3. What are you learning from your past negotiations where you didn't prepare and improvised in the moment?

Remember, don't be fooled by the obvious answer when you are curious about (C2) something. Stay with C2 as long as you need or by continuing to ask yourself "why" questions.

Whatever is coming up, have compassion toward yourself (C3). Judging or criticizing yourself prevents you from being able to behave differently.

Preparing is a sign of weakness...for your ego. The time invested in preparation will allow you to get to a deal quicker.

Now it's time to ask yourself different questions (C4) and be curious about what is coming up (C2).

1. What do you have to lose by setting time aside to prepare?
2. What could go really well if you took time to prepare?
3. What if, by preparing in a structured way, you could feel more grounded during meetings or calls and deliver better outcomes?
4. What if by preparing you could influence the way your organization conducts negotiations by sharing your experience with your colleagues?

Don't prepare for your boss or others. Do it for yourself and observe how you feel during the meetings or the calls and what the outcome is and compare it to a time when you didn't prepare. You will recuperate the time you are investing in preparation, as you will be able to pivot quickly without being paralyzed by stress.

When Your Preparation is All About You

Okay, you have decided to set time aside to prepare after reading the previous section. Great! But just being willing to prepare is only half the battle. Unfortunately, the majority of people who *do* prepare don't actually prepare *well*.

Why? Because 90% of people that prepare don't spend any time putting themselves in the other party's shoes and considering their wants and needs. Your ego wants you to focus only on yourself—your needs, desires, and goals. Your ego claims that what you want is the only thing that matters. For your ego, focusing on the other person is taking something away from you.

By focusing only on yourself or your side of the story, your strategy will likely be persuading the other side that they should come around and agree with you. You might be tempted to craft your proposal in your preparation even before meeting the other side. You will then be shocked when your counterparts don't buy into your proposal, even though there's nothing for them in it.

When you don't consider where the other party is coming from, you set yourselves up for more antagonistic and lengthy negotiations. You might claim that you want to create a partnership, but if it's all about you, it's nothing close to a partnership.

You Can't Create Value for Both Parties If It's All About You.

Let's be mindful (C1) and curious (C2) around that concept:

1. How would you react if the other party came with a proposal that didn't deliver any good for you or your company? Why?
2. What do you think you'd lose if you put yourself in the other party's shoes and tried to give them a win?
3. What are you missing when you focus only on yourself?

Take your time to explore and be curious. Don't be afraid to peel back the layers. You might not find the real answers right away as you ask any of the previous questions; your ego might want you to resist being really curious.

Bring compassion (C3) with your curiosity, as you might be judging yourself (or be upset at me!) for having to confront your ego this way. You are not a bad or selfish person for wanting to focus on yourself. It's your little voice telling you to feel that way.

Now let's look at a mindful alternative way of behaving (C4):

1. What if putting yourself in the other party's shoes will actually share your power and help you build trust?
2. What if you have better chances to structure a partnership by considering the other party's needs, constraints, and pain points?
3. What if you won't actually lose anything by considering the other person's needs?

4. What if putting yourself in the other party's shoes helps you shorten the time and complexity of the negotiation process?

As you consider these questions, you'll start to realize that considering the other side can really help the negotiation!

Write down a list of open-ended questions that you will ask the other person during your meeting or call. Use this preparation sheet as a memory jogger or cheat sheet during the session.

What are the most important elements (priorities) that will make this deal a success for you?

Do you want to demonstrate your leadership?

Do you want to demonstrate that you can bring value for your organization?

What are the most crucial factors of success for your organization?

Revenues?

Profits? If yes, how do you define profits?

Growth?

Market share?

Something else?

What does this deal mean for you, personally?

How will this deal support your credibility or reputation in your company?

If there was one aspect of this deal you can't afford to miss or lose out on, what would it be?

Observe the dynamic in your next few meetings or calls when you ask these questions. I bet you'll be pleasantly surprised!

The Power of Power

A key part of your preparation is understanding the power dynamics between your side and the other side. The perception of who has the most power in negotiation is one of the biggest concerns of negotiators.

Power in negotiation is one side's ability to influence or force the other side to give them what they want. Power is normally set by market dynamics. If you have a product or a solution nobody else offers, your side will have a lot of power.

If you are constrained by time and need a deal right away, your side might find itself with less power.

Power is a function of the business environment. But your ego doesn't see it that way. It will tell you that the notion of power is personal. According to your ego, it's *you* that doesn't have much power (or has a lot). In both cases, this is a perception of the reality instead of the reality itself...but because this personal notion of power is ego-driven, power dynamics bring up a *lot* of emotions. Which means that how you feel about the power dynamics of a negotiation is something you need to prepare for with mindfulness.

When You Feel You Don't Have Much Power

When you feel you have no power, you let fear of being overpowered drive you. When you prepare to negotiate from that perspective, you'll approach the negotiation out of fear that you need the other side more than they need you. You're afraid of upsetting the other side, damaging your relationship with them, or simply getting a really bad deal.

Feeling you have no power influences what you want and how far you are prepared to go in the terms of the negotiation itself. You will likely negotiate with yourself during your preparation—i.e., telling yourself there's no way the other side will give you what you want, and might even get upset if you ask for that much, so you should ask for less—before the meeting even starts.

Preparing in this mindset of fear will also set you up to behave submissively in the meeting. Instead of asking thought-provoking questions designed to make the other side seriously consider what they're offering, you'll ask simplistic, yes-or-no questions that invite stonewalling. Instead of stating your needs assertively, you will ask the other side for permission to have those needs met. This strategy undermines your position and sets the other side up to walk all over you. From this ego-driven perspective, it's easy for the ego to feel defensive and pressured, to justify giving in, and to feel a need to placate the other side.

If you let this feeling of lack of power take control, you will not be happy with the outcome. And you will dread the next negotiation as that lack of power will be even more pronounced next time!

Let's bring mindfulness to help you experience what is happening and why is it happening (C1) and be curious around this perception of lack of power (C2)

1. What are you afraid will happen because you have less power? Why?
2. What/who are you trying to protect?
3. How is this feeling of lack of power related to other aspects of your life?

When we feel we don't have power in negotiation, it is often related to the same feeling in our personal life. To allow yourself to really connect with that sense of powerlessness, I encourage you to go deeper with the previous questions focusing on your personal life.

Connect with self-compassion (C3). It's not easy to realize and admit that you don't have power (or feel like you don't). You are not alone. Feeling powerless is very common. Powerlessness is an emotion sent by your ego to get you to try and protect yourself at all costs. But the truth is that most negotiators underestimate their own power and overestimate the other side's power. So even if you feel powerless, you most likely aren't! Even if the other side seems to have more power, you aren't doomed to fail from the outset.

Most importantly, no matter how little power you feel you have, you can still have a successful negotiation. If you prepare well, you will increase your power going into the negotiation—and may well take back some power from the other side! Being mindful in the meeting to be in control of your emotions also helps, as it allows you to hold onto power when your ego wants to give it away (and be ready if the other side's ego makes them give power away).

Realizing that you have more power than you think you have leads to better outcomes.

Let's go through the C4 step to explore how you can change your feeling of lack of power:

1. What if the feeling of lack of power was just your perception (and the other person might feel the same)? How might you determine that?

2. What if the negotiation wasn't yours to lead but led by one of your colleagues, what would be the impact on your sense of the power balance? Looking at it from an outside perspective helps you see the power balance more clearly without letting your ego get in the way.

3. What if you could shift the notion of power in your favor by being mindful during the meeting?

4. How is your notion of power evolving after exploring these questions?

Don't let fear drive your preparation. The lack of power you feel is strictly your little voice saying so. It's not the reality.

When You Feel You Have All the Power

The flip side of power is when you feel like you have more than the other side—where you think they need you more than you need them. In this position, you might think you can impose your will on them and make them give you whatever you want. But beware: this feeling comes from your ego too, and so it's still more perception than reality.

From this perspective, you may not bother taking the time to prepare, as you know what you want and are convinced you can overpower the other side. If you do take the time to prepare, you'll unconsciously prepare to be overly optimistic and dominant. It's easy for the ego to feel overconfident or cocky and to justify persuasion and even aggression when you feel entitled to get what you want.

Problem is, when you strongly impose your will on the other side, your approach is very rigid. You'll most likely ask for extreme terms with very little flexibility, which means you'll have a hard time actually getting what you want. And if you're in your ego around having more power, but you aren't getting what you want, you'll likely get emotional and may end up damaging your relationship with the other side. (Not to mention you'll come off as a jerk!)

If you think you have more power, you might not feel like being mindful. But mindfulness will help you here—a lot more than you think. Connect with yourself (C1) and be curious (C2) around the origin or the source of this entitlement to overpower the other side.

1. What are you trying to prove to yourself? To others?
2. What are you afraid will happen if you don't overpower others?
3. How is this perception of overpowering others relate to other aspects of your life?

As with the idea of having less power, the notion of having power over other people doesn't always manifest exclusively in business. It's often related to your way of being in your personal life. Allow yourself time to explore the previous questions both in the context of work **and** personal life. **Keep asking yourself "why" each time you connect with an answer. Your ego might be very resistant to explore the notion of overpowering as it's afraid to give any power away.**

It's easy to feel threatened by the idea of losing power—what you have, you want to defend! So, bring some compassion (C3) to these feelings of defensiveness around power. No one's saying you're a bully or a bad person for having more power than the other side. More importantly, no one's saying that you'll fail at negotiation or lose what you want if you actually have less power (or don't use your power to take the other side for everything they have). It's okay to try different approaches besides overpowering the other side. You can choose to use your power for good, to create value for both parties and make sure everyone gets what they want.

Because here's the truth: the need to overpower the other side is 100% your ego talking.

The Best Negotiators Get What They Want Without Bullying or Overpowering the Other Side.

Instead, they know they can get great results and still care about the other person and the relationship, even when they assert their needs and goals. You don't have to be disrespectful or mean to be a good negotiator or even a tough one.

Let's bring C4 in and explore other choices of behavior:

1. What if you didn't have to overpower others to get what you want?
2. If the other side has better ideas that actually get you more of what you want, does that actually take power away from you?
3. What if the other side actually has more power than you think? How will that change your approach?
4. How can you use your power to create value for both sides?

Don't let your ego control your approach. Eventually, you will find yourself in a position where you don't have that much power, and then you'll appreciate the other side opting *not* to overpower you.

Now that we covered your internal mindset during preparation, let's explore preparation situations where you will have to deal with your internal team.

When You Need Alignment and Your Internal Team Is In Their Ego

Before meeting with the other party, you may need to get in alignment with your internal team. Your internal team certainly includes your boss and may also include members of other departments that support sales, like marketing, finance, and contracting. These people won't usually tell you specifically what to say in the negotiation, but they will have a say—sometimes the deciding say—in the terms you're able to offer. Their guidance will be helpful because they know the organizations priorities, areas of flexibility, and hard limits, often better than you will.

As you prepare to sit down with them, be advised that your internal team members are most likely already in their egos. They want to win, to get the maximum they can. Marketing will claim that your product/solution is better than anybody else's so it's worth an extreme price. Finance has set a budget that might not be realistic for the environment in which you compete. Your boss is prioritizing looking good for his boss by closing an aggressive deal. It's all about them.

It's also a common assumption for your internal team to believe that you can get literally everything they want—and that you can do it in one meeting. Because they don't usually negotiate in their own work tasks, they tend to think negotiation is easy and don't understand why you can't deliver better deals. Their egos tell them that *they* could get any deal they want, giving them a false sense of superiority and making them want to distrust you.

Because these team members are in their egos, they will do and say a lot of things that will make it harder for you to prepare well. They may recommend coming to the table with a very extreme offer, not realizing that doing so will likely upset the other side and add a lot of time to the negotiation. They may try to avoid giving you a hard limit for what you can offer, either out of fear that you'll just offer that amount to the other side to close the deal quickly, or because they can't afford to walk away and will take any deal you can strike. They may waffle on giving you clear priorities, because they don't realize (or care) that getting absolutely everything you want is like a snow leopard—it exists, but it's so rare that only a very few people living have ever seen one.

It can be quite a challenging conversation and internal negotiation. But just because they may be in their egos, doesn't mean you have to be. Mindfulness will help you get through it.

Let's pause and focus on yourself (C1) and be curious (C2) about what is going inside of you:

1. What are you afraid of or concerned about when you meet with your internal team?
2. What are you protecting by not challenging them on what they want from you?
3. What is the impact of your feeling that they don't trust you?

Bring self-compassion (C3) to this moment, as you might judge yourself or be upset at yourself or your company. Don't worry. You are not the only one experiencing these situations. Just about everyone who has to get information from an internal team encounters these issues.

When you challenge your internal team with mindfulness and respect, you are building your credibility in their eyes.

Let's bring the last step of C4U™ to explore potential choices for behaving differently:

1. What if your team is more scared than you are because they don't feel they are in control of the negotiation?
2. What if gaining internal alignment can give you more power in the negotiation by defining your path forward?
3. What if challenging them to prioritize the variables, to set a starting point that is not extreme, and to set a limit, would help you build your credibility and demonstrate that you have a plan?
4. What can you say to help them feel comfortable giving you specific terms, priorities, and/or limits?

Being mindful when meeting with your internal team is essential for both you and them. If you are in your ego and they are in their ego, most likely, they will be frustrated, and you will be as well as you won't get clarity on the alignment. Your internal team wants to believe that you have a plan for your negotiation and, therefore, are in control of driving the negotiation. If you can stand up to them without your ego taking over, they will be more likely to trust you.

o————o

Now that we have covered preparation for yourself and your team, let's explore preparation situations where you will have to deal with an external party.

When You Need to Plan to Handle Emotions: Yours and Theirs

As we now know very clearly, negotiation has nothing to do with being rational. Negotiations are, most of the time, ego-driven. No matter how prepared you are skill-wise or how much effort you are putting in to be logical, emotions will come up (yours and theirs) and make rational thought really hard to hold onto. So, getting ready for when emotions come up on either side of the table will be key to successful preparation.

The best way to be ready to manage emotions during calls or meetings is to include mindfulness in your preparation. Not only will practicing the C4U™ system ahead of time set you up to use it during upcoming meetings, but many of the same emotions that come up during the meetings will also come up during your preparation.

Practicing managing your emotions starts with experiencing and understanding those emotions in a safe space where there are no real stakes. The best way to experience emotions that could show up in a meeting way is to explore them in the preparation with what-if scenarios:

What if they threaten to walk away if you don't agree with them?

What if they are upset or angry, and they yell at you?

What if you can't get what you want?

What if they reject your proposal, and you have to ask your boss for additional flexibility?

What other scenarios could trigger your emotions?

As you experience each emotion, allow yourself to be fully aware of everything that is coming up inside of you (C1). It is crucial here that you don't stay in your head and rationalize what you feel. Be curious (C2) about these emotions to understand where they are coming from:

1. What emotions are coming up around this scenario?
2. What other aspects of your life are triggering the same emotions?
3. What else (e.g. judgments, other emotions or sensations) is coming up around these emotions?

If you are experiencing challenges connecting with answers, you might want to ask the same questions about a specific situation in your personal life. You might encounter less resistance this way.

Connect with compassion (C3) as there's nothing wrong with you for being triggered or feeling an emotion you don't want. Remember, we are all emotional creatures. Whatever is coming up is okay. Judging or criticizing yourself will only move you further away from making real contact with that part of yourself.

Planning in advance to handle emotions will allow you to be your best in the moment.

Now look at the emotion from the C4 step, and determine what you can change when it comes up.

1. What can you learn about experiencing that emotion?
2. Who says that is the way you are and can't change?
3. What is your history with that emotion and what would it take to gain some freedom from it?
4. What if you could minimize your instinctual emotional response and be in the moment, in control of the situation, and able to pivot without your ego reacting?

When you become aware of your emotional triggers ahead of time, you can give yourself tools and tactics to handle them before you actually *need* to. This sets you up to control your ego and emotions rather than letting them control you in the moments where that control matters most. And that works whether the emotions are on your side, the other side, or both.

Being mindful and in control of your emotions is the ability to be your best and deliver better outcomes—without your ego dictating your behavior.

When You Have to Deliver Bad News

Often, as Alexis did in her first meeting with Lucas, our job is to deliver bad news to the other side: we can't accept their offer, we need to charge them more, we don't have any more time, we can't give them 100% of our business, etc. While practicing mindfulness can help prepare us to deliver bad news in general, there's a more specific part of the delivery that needs its own prep work: the words you use to deliver it.

Language is an interesting side of mindfulness because it's often something we let our ego control without meaning to.

Have you ever prepared to say something really firmly (maybe to stand up for yourself) or to share something the other person doesn't want to hear, but then in the moment found yourself saying it really timidly instead?

This is your ego bringing up fear of upsetting the other person or triggering a negative reaction. Instead of focusing on delivering the news itself, you're focusing on being afraid of how the other side will react to that news. Your ego has tricked you into saying the same message you came to deliver in a completely different, and rarely helpful, way.

Specifically, your ego will often use these softer and submissive words and phrases:

- If you are okay with it…
- I wish…
- I hope…
- It would be nice…
- I would love/I would like…
- We'll try…
- If possible…

The problem when you communicate this way is that you look insecure, timid, perhaps even asking for permission. You've just invited the other side to put pressure on you to make the bad news less bad for them—and worse for you.

Delivering bad news is definitely stressful, but mindfulness will help. Let's take a moment to focus inward (C1) and be curious about this concept of being afraid of delivering bad news(C2):

1. What is happening inside of you when you know you have to deliver bad news?

2.   What is that emotion telling you about yourself?

3.   Where else in your life does that emotion manifest itself?

4.   What do you feel is at risk when you deliver bad news?

Remember to stay curious and follow up after the first answers you get. Don't let your ego stop you at the surface—dive deep!

Don't let self-judgment or inner critic ruin this moment. Have compassion (C3) for yourself. Nobody else is judging or criticizing you. Know that you aren't alone in feeling nervous around delivering bad news or expressing yourself assertively—*everyone* gets nervous about doing that, including the people across the table from you! It's okay to be afraid of upsetting the other side. But you don't have to let that fear control what you need *or* how you ask for it.

Let's consider other choices (C4):

1.   What if there was a way to express yourself with more confident language without being afraid of the person's reaction?

2.   What if you could be clear and direct when delivering bad news and not feel like a bad person?

3.   How could you deliver bad news with compassion and clarity rather than fear?

4.   How could you be clear about your needs while still respecting and acknowledging the other side's needs?

5.   What is your personal history with this emotion? What would it take to gain freedom from it?

The Key is Not the Bad News Itself But How You Deliver It.

When delivering bad news, you want to position yourself as equal to the other person. You want to sound confident and assertive. Being assertive is expressing your needs clearly without fearing the other person's reaction. Assertiveness is being respectful of the other person but isn't looking to them for approval, permission, or validation. An assertive negotiator knows what they want and is prepared to ask for it. And contrary to what your ego will tell you, being assertive will not hurt your relationship with the other side or your chances for a successful negotiation.

Being Assertive Doesn't Damage the Relationship.

Assertive language sounds like:

- I want…
- I have to…
- I'll need…
- We can't…
- We must…
- It is imperative…
- It is not sustainable…

Do you feel the difference between this assertive language and the previous list? You are not asking for permission. Your focus is on delivering bad news, not on the other person's potential reaction.

Your ego will balk at using assertive language—it will blame you for the other person's reaction.

Your ego wants you to believe that telling the other side what you can't do for them or what you want in a confident and assertive way will damage the relationship.

In my experience, when people use assertive language, they don't get a lot of pushback from the other side. When you speak with assertive language, the other party can sense the confidence and energy and realize they have very little chance to push back and make you downplay the bad news.

Here are four practices to help you prepare for delivering bad news mindfully:

1. You know your ego will try to hijack the way you deliver the news. Mindfully write down word for word what you want to share and practice saying it out loud until you feel comfortable doing so. Read it to a colleague and ask for feedback on tone, conciseness, and choice of

words, so you can build your confidence in delivering the right message with the right tone.

2. Plan for the other person to have a negative emotional response and try to identify what your emotions may be at that moment. As mentioned above, your ego is going to blame you for their reaction. Unless your intent is to hurt someone, *you are not responsible for their reaction or response*. It's their ego reacting. You'll still show empathy and compassion toward their emotion, but you won't back off the bad news you just delivered. You cannot control others, only yourself and your reactions.

When You are Delivering Bad News, You Don't Own the Other Side's Reaction.

3. Your ego wants you to hold off as long as you can when delivering bad news. The longer it can put off someone reacting to you, the better. But put yourself in the other side's shoes for a moment. If you have to receive bad news from your counterpart, when do you want to hear about it? Early on or two months down the road after a lot of time and energy have been spent working on the project? I bet you'd want to know it as soon as possible. If they waited till the last minute to deliver it, you might even feel betrayed or misled. Prepare to deliver the bad news as early as possible in the negotiation. That way you'll have as much time as possible to find a creative solution.

4. The best way to get what you want and mitigate the impact of the bad news is to offer flexibility elsewhere in the negotiation terms. For example, you might say that you need to reevaluate the contract, but that you value the relationship you have with the other side and are willing to consider different options that will work for both sides. Flexibility elsewhere supports your intent of getting what you want and finding a solution that is mutually agreeable. Prepare some areas of flexibility you could bring to the table along with the bad news.

Finally, if your counterpart interrupts your delivery of the bad news with an angry reaction, trying to bully you into backing off, stay present (C1). It's their ego reacting. Remember, you are not responsible for their emotions. Slow down your breathing. You are stronger than they want you to think you are (C3). It's not the time to back off from your bad news. Ask them to let you finish (C4). If they don't let you talk, let them finish and then call out their behavior (C4). You might say, "I understand you are upset or frustrated, but by being aggressive, you are putting yourself in a position where you can't hear me and finding a solution is going to be more challenging."

While they are in their ego and emotional; you must stay calm and mindful. Acknowledge their emotion, finish what you wanted to share, and let them know that you are prepared to work with them to find a solution that will work for both of you.

Alexis Goes Over Her Preparation with Mia

"Let's review what you're planning for the meeting with Lucas tomorrow. What's your strategy?" said Mia four days later.

"My strategy is to try and create value for both of us, based on what I know about his company and how much we need each other."

"How will you deliver the bad news that your side of things hasn't changed much?"

"I'll be upfront about it and tell him what is and isn't workable on our end and then go into asking what would be valuable for him from there."

"What will you do if he gets emotional with you?"

"I'll remember that his emotions don't apply to me, that I don't have to be upset just because he is."

"What if he gets angry or contemptuous?"

"I'll be present with what I'm feeling come up in response, and I'll remind myself that it's okay to feel it but that it doesn't control me."

"What if he starts yelling again?"

"I'll go as deep into C4U™ as I can, and try to make a different choice than I did last time."

"Good!" said Mia. "How are you feeling about this plan?"

"Nervous," said Alexis. "Really nervous. But I'm going to keep C4U™ with me and do my best, and I think I'm ready to do that much at least."

"I'd say you are, too," said Mia. "I'm looking forward to hearing how it goes."

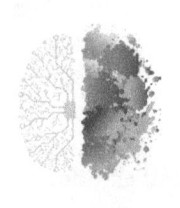

Chapter 7
MINDFULLY STARTING YOUR CLIMB

"The summit is what drives us, but the climb itself is what matters."
—Conrad Anker

Alexis Faces Off With Lucas

When Alexis arrived in the conference room the next morning, Lucas was already there, gulping coffee and scribbling in a notepad. He didn't look up when Alexis stepped inside.

"Good morning," she ventured. "Any of that coffee left?"

Lucas grunted and waved one hand in the direction of a sideboard, where coffee and bagels were arranged. Alexis fixed a cup for herself and sat down across from Lucas, who turned a new page and continued to write as if she weren't there.

"Um…okay, Lucas, I'm ready whenever you are," she said, opening her briefcase and laying out notes in front of her. Lucas held up one finger in the "wait a minute" gesture and finished two more lines before putting the pen down and finally looking up at Alexis.

"Alright, now that's done. I've only got a few minutes here, Alexa, so why don't you tell me what you've come up with that's different from two weeks ago." He sat back and steepled his fingers, waiting.

Alexis took a deep breath, already feeling panic rising in her chest. "Okay, well, first of all, it's Alexis, not Alexa. And second, as you remember from our last meeting, the goal is to have your company renew its overdue contract with us so we can keep working together. So, I've talked with my team, and unfortunately, we're not going to be able to continue the discount we've given your company up until now, but if it's okay with you, we're prepared to offer you five percent below what was proposed in the previous offer if you sign a three-year contract today—"

"Okay, I'm going to stop you right there," said Lucas. "Look, last time I told you to go sharpen your pencil and bring me something I could work with. What have you been doing for the last two weeks? Five percent off your previous offer is a bunch of crap! I made it perfectly clear that we can't pay any more than we're paying now."

Alexis swallowed hard. "Lucas, I know you said that, but your company has been paying below market value for the entire length of the last contract, not to mention for the last four months past the initial renewal date. No one else has this level of discount that you've had for the last six years. We can't honor these prices anymore! So, you and I need to come up with something that gives both of us value we can work with."

"Both of us?" Lucas laughed. "Why should I care what you get out of this? You don't care about what I'm getting! We're both here to screw each other over, and right now, I've got the bigger screwdriver. Either you bring me a proposal I can work with, or my company will go across the street."

Alexis felt her face flush, and her hands start to shake. "You know very well what you have been paying. You think our competition will propose a contract like yours with that big of a discount? They'd be out of business in six months! You need us as much as we need you!"

Lucas leaned over the table so that his face was only a foot or so from Alexis's. "The h** we do!" he hissed. "Now, I'm going to give you one more minute to come up with something I like, and after that, I'm walking out of this room!"

Fighting to keep her composure, Alexis felt the room start to go gray again. No! *she thought frantically,* I've forgotten all about C4U™ —how did I screw this up so badly so fast?

"I'm waiting!" said Lucas, tapping his foot impatiently.

Terror, that's what this is, *thought Alexis*. Sheer terror. I'm terrified. Why? Because if I don't fix this somehow, I'm going to lose this account for real this time, and Jorge is going to throw me out of the leadership program.

Alexis felt completely lost, like everything Mia had taught her had blown away in a gust of wind. You had this just yesterday! *she berated herself.* What is wrong with you, Alexis? You've got to save this deal right now, and you can't even remember what to do! You're such an idiot!

"Any time now!" Lucas was staring at her as she seemingly stared out into space.

"Listen," she blurted, *"This is the best pricing we can offer you for the volume you need, and we even added a year onto the offer just for you. You're the only client with such an offer on the table." Alexis added with a mix of impatience and despair.*

"I can't commit to three years, and I need better pricing!" yelled Lucas.

"Wait a second!" said Alexis, realizing something suddenly. "You never mentioned anything about the length of the contract before. The additional 5% discount in this revised proposal came with a three-year contract instead of two. But now you tell me that you still want better pricing without committing for three years. Why does the length of the contract matter to you?"

"Because I said it does." Lucas was clearly annoyed. "I need to get better pricing without committing for three years, and that's just the way it is. Now, I need to run to another meeting. Are you going to give me what I want, or am I going across the street this afternoon?"

Alexis grabbed at the one straw she could think of. "Look, Lucas, it's obvious to me that we aren't going to agree today, but that doesn't mean we have to throw away years of our companies working together, does it? We can solve this; we just need more time to explore how we can create a solution we both want. So, I propose we take the next two months to figure out a new contract that we both are actually happy with."

Lucas stopped halfway to the door. "Okay, suppose we do that. What am I supposed to tell my boss in the meantime?"

Alexis mentally crossed her fingers, hoping this would work. "Tell him he gets to keep the current contract terms during that time, but after that, the costs will revert to list price unless you and I come up with a contract we're all happy with."

"He might not buy that," said Lucas. "He might just tell me to go across the street."

"And then you'd be having the same problems there, except that instead of having an established relationship with a company who values your account, you'd be trying to talk down a new supplier who has no reason to care about anything except how much money they can get out of you. I can't see how that's an improvement."

Lucas sighed. "Alright, fine. Call me in a month and let me know what you've got."

"Actually, that's not what I meant," said Alexis, surprising herself by sounding far more assertive than she felt. "Coming up with this contract will take both of us working together. We need to meet again next week, and we need to be completely open with each other about what we both need. That's the only way to create something that will make both our companies happy."

Lucas looked skeptical. "That's not how we've worked with your company before."

"I know," said Alexis, "and based on our conversation today, I think that's the problem."

Lucas looked at her for a long moment. Somehow Alexis held his gaze, even as her insides started shaking.

Finally, Lucas gave a short nod. "Fine. Set it up." Then he turned and left.

Alexis dropped into her chair, completely exhausted.

o———————o

Preparation is the foundation you need for a successful negotiation. But you can't just prepare forever—eventually you actually have to have the first meeting or two. Let's look at three situations early in the negotiation process where your ego will want to take over.

When Someone Has to Make the First Proposal

As you now know, your ego will try to take over in every phase of negotiation. But there's something about the first proposal meeting that really puts the ego into overdrive. Maybe it's because this meeting has the first real moment of competition in it (i.e., which of you gets to speak first). Maybe the stakes feel real for the first time. Maybe there's pressure to accomplish something right away. Maybe it's all of those things.

The only way to climb the mountain is to pick a path and start climbing. In negotiation, it's the same thing: someone has to deliver the first proposal. Who should it be—your side or the other side?

To be fair, sometimes you already know the answer to that question. In Alexis's scenario, it was clear to both her and Lucas that making the first proposal was her job. If you already know that going first is your responsibility, or that there's an expectation that the other side will go first, great. But if it's unclear who's supposed to start, or if either of you could, you've got a decision to make—a decision your ego is going to try to influence.

Proposing first usually conveys that you want to establish power or gain dominance over the other side. It also anchors you to a starting position (giving the other side more work to do), and it lets you start the negotiation with your terms and numbers rather than theirs. This positions you in control of the negotiation and pre-frames the other side to follow your lead.

On the other hand, purposefully going second allows you to shape the flow of the negotiation by responding to what the other side gives you, shows you where your opponent stands before you have to show them anything, and lets them set the limits of the negotiation for you. If you are able to quickly pivot in response to them, this takes some pressure off of you and allows you to adapt more easily.

In reality, either option can be workable for you, and you can decide which works better based on your preparation. But your ego is going to want you to decide based on your emotions.

From your ego's perspective, going first feels dominant and aggressive, like you're beating the other side before the race has even started. If your ego really wants to win, it's going to push you to go first—and urge you to judge yourself and feel like a failure if the other side beats you to the punch.

On the other hand, your ego might be afraid of going first and screwing it up. If your ego really doesn't want to risk antagonizing the other side or making a mistake, it's going to push you to let the other side go first— and urge you to doubt yourself and feel weak if the other side insists you go first.

When your ego makes the decision, it turns a situation where either option could help into a situation where both options will hurt you.

Let's pause for a moment (C1) and bring curiosity (C2) to these questions. Review the last few negotiations you were involved in:

If you went first:
1. Did going first support your approach (remember, going first is a way to gain power and dominance)?
2. How did the other side react?
3. How did the rest of the negotiation go?

If they went first:
1. Did you prepare for them to go first?
   a.   If not, what prevented you planning this scenario?
2. What was your emotion at that moment?
3. What was the impact of that emotion for the rest of the meeting? The negotiation?
4. What is your favorite approach: going first or letting them go first?
5. What can you learn from your preference?

You might feel a mix bag of emotions. There is nothing to do here, just being present with compassion (C3) It's not the time to judge.

Imagine that you can be comfortable and in control (C4) regardless who goes first.

1. What if by being curious and calm you actually negate their intent of gaining advantage over you?
2. What if you can gain power back by asking good negotiation questions about their proposal?

As mentioned earlier, making the first proposal that early in the negotiation process, is likely ego driven. That proposal originates from the preparation itself without any input from the other side. There is a high risk of being rejected as these proposals are normally design at their most extreme position.

This first proposal is not designed to close the deal. It might sound like it, but in general negotiators don't start the negotiation with their final and less desirable position. Remember, the intent behind it is to intimidate the other side. It's you advantage to ask as many questions as you can around that proposal to really understand what's behind that proposal and separate wants and needs. If you make the first proposal, you should expect the other side to be curious around your own proposal as well.

When Your Proposal Is All About You

Let's say that you have decided to go first. When you design and deliver a first proposal, your ego is going to sound a lot like a two-year-old: "ME! ME! ME!" In order to get what it wants, your ego will urge you to make a proposal that's all about you because it wants to win. This is Jorge's tactic—go first and slam the other side with a proposal that gets you the most while giving the other side the least.

But making a proposal that is all about you doesn't create value for both sides—which means it will put the other side into *their* ego. Going first and letting your ego control the content of the proposal is one of the most frequent situations that can derail a negotiation.

When Your Ego Is In the Driver Seat, Your First Proposal Is All About You, Inviting the Other Side to Wear Their boxing Gloves and Let Their Own Ego Fight Back.

Let's pause here (C1) and be curious (C2) around making and delivering the first proposal:

1. In your proposal, what is the value for the other side? What do they get out of what you offer?
2. How would you react if you were receiving this exact proposal from the other side?

3. Did you position your proposal at an extreme scenario (a scenario you can't defend or that the market won't support)?
4. Did you go into this meeting expecting to close the deal today?

What is coming up for you as you consider these questions? Do you want to deny you actually made it all about you? Are you judging yourself? Do you feel embarrassed?

Whatever the emotions and feelings coming up for you, connect with compassion (C3). Nobody is saying that you are a bad negotiator. Most negotiators simply deliver the first proposal they prepared in their initial preparation without asking the other side any additional questions—like Alexis was doing at the beginning of her story. Making it all about you is an ego-driven decision, which means that even if you've done it before (or even just did it a moment ago) you don't have to do it again.

Let's explore mindful choices (C4) to approach making your proposal differently:

1. What if, by gathering information about the other side, you could create something interesting and valuable for both parties without losing your power?
2. What if, by using this information, you could build trust with the other side and make the rest of the negotiation smoother and more efficient?
3. What if, by being mindful with your first proposal, you could help your counterpart avoid being controlled by their ego?
4. What if, by understanding the needs and pain points of the other side, you could craft a proposal that's actually *more* likely to get you what you want?

When You Are Told Something, You Don't Want to Hear

Now let's say you decide to go second, and the other side's proposal isn't good for you. Or say you still went first, but the first thing the other side said in response was "no way!"

Not getting what you want or what you were expecting, or being directly told "no," are among the biggest triggers for your ego. Whether the other side is giving you bad terms, denying you something you want, or rejecting your first proposal, if you aren't prepared, your ego's instinctual response will take over before you know it.

By now you know what that feels like—your stress level goes up, your emotions shove rational thought out of your head, and you don't feel in control anymore. More specifically, you might connect with fear of personal rejection, a sense of failure, anger at the other side, and/or fear of losing the deal.

Whichever emotions you are experiencing, you'll sense a power shift in favor of the other person. They've just staked a position that says they have more power than you—the party who can more easily say no is normally the party with the most power. So, your ego will want to grab that power back! Usually that means either responding with aggression (defending your proposal or attacking the other side's refusal) or persuasion (explaining your proposal in more detail or simply repeating it) in the hope that the other side will give you back the power.

Unfortunately, neither of those tactics work well. In the face of your own emotions, the other side will likely get emotional as well as their own egos start to feel threatened. So, they'll respond to your aggression with aggression of their own, and to your persuasion with stonewalling. Meanwhile, both sides have lost all clarity of thought and have no way to find a creative solution together.

Let's stop here for a moment (C1) and be curious (C2) about what is going on internally:

1. What is coming up as you hear something you didn't want to hear?
2. How is this bad news impacting your confidence?
3. How is this bad news influencing the commitment you already made to your internal team or your external counterpart?
4. What is that bad news is taking away from you?
5. What can't you get now that you wanted to get—and what can you potentially still get?

You can do this C2 set of questions in two stages: first, go through them with focus on a specific work situation; and second, think of a specific personal life situation that happened in the past. (Alternately, you might want to explore one question at a time and consider it under both work and personal life angles and see what is coming up.) **Most likely, your ego's reactions when you are told something you don't want to hear originate from when you were a kid.**

You might experience a wide variety of emotions and feelings here. Connect with self-compassion (C3). Don't push back on that emotion, and don't judge yourself. Everyone struggles when they don't get what they want or what they expected. **Continue being curious about it.**

Let's be curious about the potential reasons why the other side rejected your proposal:

1. Did your proposal stake out extreme position (one the other side can't possibly meet or that the market won't justify)?
2. Did your proposal deliver value for them? How do you know?
3. Did you deliver the proposal aggressively, trying to dominate or intimidate the other side? Alternately, did you deliver it submissively, trying to ask their permission?
4. Was your proposal all about you?

Again, connect with compassion (C3) if you feel like you are judging or criticizing yourself. Getting rejected hurts—for everyone, not just for you! You're not alone in having to learn that, or to learn how to deal with it constructively.

Let's use C4 to help you figure out how to respond to this rejection successfully:

1. What if this rejection means you are not getting what you want but are still getting what you really need?
2. What if having your proposal rejected isn't personal to you, and so you don't actually need to feel personally rejected?

3. What if there were other options besides full acceptance and full rejection?

4. What if you can be creative with those options and find a solution both sides like?

5. What if their rejection is actually the beginning of something even better than what got rejected?

By being mindful and using the C4 pillar, you can move beyond the rejection and see what else is possible.

When you are told something, you don't want to hear, it's not about just accepting it and doing nothing about it. It's about mastering your emotions and using creativity to create a different path or strategy to give you what you really need. This way, everything is not lost, like your ego wants you to believe, and you can pivot and still be in control.

When the Other Side Is Using Time In Their Favor

Time is always a factor in negotiations, but it tends to have the biggest impact at the beginning and at the end—the two times where one side or the other is most in a hurry to close a deal!

There are two early-on situations where the other side might use time in their favor: when they drag their feet about making a decision and when they put pressure on you to respond within a specific timeframe. Lucas did both of these with Alexis—his company initially kept asking for one-month contract extensions to avoid having to make a new contract, but when Alexis proposed taking more time to work out a new contract, suddenly Lucas was in a hurry to finish right away!

Let's look at the first option. Let's say the other side is dragging their feet to make a decision, not responding to your emails for days at a time, or even asking for multiple extensions on the negotiation (and/or the contract itself). You may become frustrated, impatient, or angry with them. You might also worry that they're talking to a competitor.

Before your emotions develop further, let's pause for a moment (C1) and be curious about what is going on inside of you (C2):

1. What emotions are coming up for you in response to this tactic? Why are they coming up?
2. What do you feel is in your power or control at this moment?
3. Which brings up more emotion: your counterpart taking their time or your internal team rushing you? Is the other side really what's causing you to feel the way you do?
4. What is at stake for you if the negotiation takes more time? How will you feel if that happens?

Don't forget to bring compassion (C3) as you feel into these emotions. Whatever you experience, it is okay.

Let's explore other ways of looking at this scenario (C4). One way is to consider the time factor from a different angle.

1. What if the fact that they are dragging their feet has nothing to with you?
2. What if the delay in their response doesn't mean that your business is at risk?
3. What if you can take control of the situation and help them come to a quicker decision?
4. What if the negotiation just needs to take the time that it takes, and both sides will be okay when it does?

Considering questions like these are important because right about now, your ego will want you to vent your frustration and worry on the other side. So, before you do that, use these questions to help yourself understand your ego's explanation of events probably isn't the real one.

The other side might be overwhelmingly busy, short-staffed, or facing other internal issues that prevent them from moving faster. They may be unclear on what they want to ask for, or what they can offer you. They could even be doing extra preparation work to bring back their best offer. Could they also be using time to mess with you? Sure. But by choosing to respond with empathy rather than frustration, you'll let them know that the situation is not triggering you.

So instead of asking (or demanding) what's taking so long, try open-ended questions like:

What's preventing them from moving forward right now?

What can you do to support them in their process?

What's happening in their world right now that you don't know about?

What would make this easier for them?

When you are curious and want to understand them, they will usually respond positively—even if they really can't speed things up.

Another option is to employ "carrot and stick" tactics to try to get the other side moving. If you offer to give them an extra 5% discount if they close the deal within two weeks, that's a carrot. If you tell them you'll take their company's preferential pricing off the table if they don't close the deal within two weeks, that's a stick.

Carrots and sticks can be helpful for moving slow negotiators along, but they aren't always reliable, and they can easily get hijacked by your ego. People tend to respond positively to carrots at first, but over time can start to expect them no matter what, which puts you in a bad spot because now your ego is attached to using them to get what it wants. Sticks are even tougher to rely on—they may sound threatening, but you have to be willing to back them up with action, even if that action may hurt your working relationship. If you're not willing to do that (and many people aren't, especially when their egos bring fear into the equation!), the stick becomes an empty threat and your credibility drops. So, feel free to explore these options, but do it carefully.

One final option is to use your own initiative to expedite the process. Instead of asking for their agreement with an offer, tell them that unless you hear from them by a certain date, you'll assume they agree. Trust me, they'll be sure to reply by that date if they don't!

Now let's discuss the other situation, where they pressure you with time to make a decision. They sent you an RFP (request for proposal) and give you a ridiculously short amount of time to answer (say, 1-3 days) to complete and return it to them. Or maybe they give you their offer, but say you have to accept it within 24 hours or it's off the table.

These scenarios trigger your ego for the opposite reason: instead of things going too slow, now suddenly they're going too fast! It can feel like the other side is putting a gun in your face and counting to ten before pulling the trigger. Your ego goes into fight-or-flight mode, you drown in fear of losing the deal, and you don't know what to do except maybe give in.

Let's mute the external world for a moment (C1) and be curious about what is going on inside of you (C2);

1. What are the consequences of this aggressive timeline? What are you afraid will happen if you don't meet it?
2. What emotions are coming up around having to move so fast?
3. How do you define the power dynamics in this moment? Does feeling rushed make you feel powerless?
4. When else in your life have you been forced to make rushed decisions? What happened then? How did you feel about it?

Remember to take your time to fully explore the answers to these questions, as you might experience multiple emotions. You might even judge yourself for feeling them. This is your ego reacting, don't let it take things over. Be compassionate (C3) and accept what is coming up. No one is judging you here.

As a way to behave differently than your ego wants, use the C4 pillar to help you explore different choices or options:

1. What if using time in their favor was purely an aggressive tactic for them to get what they want? What if they actually have plenty of time?
2. What if their emotional tactic didn't have to throw you off balance?
3. What if you can call out what they're doing, deflect their threats and gain control back?
4. What if standing up for taking the time you need actually builds more trust and balances power better than moving as fast as they want?

In the vast majority of situations, forcing you to make a decision fast is purely an emotional tactic to make you give in. It's a tactic that aggressive negotiators use to gain power by putting pressure on you. They believe you are scared and vulnerable, and so they use time to get additional concessions from your side.

Remember the story of my negotiation in Japan in Chapter 3. The customers waited until right before I had to leave to catch my flight back to North America, then told me I needed to decide on whether or not their proposed price increase would work before I left. This was clearly using time in their favor. If I only had a few minutes to make that crucial decision, they bet that I'd cave and take a bad deal rather than make my company pay for another Japan trip down the line.

When your ego wants you to give in, the courageous choice (C4) is to call out what's happening from an observer's point of view. For example, in response to their demand you could ask questions like:

> What is the reason behind this time pressure to make a decision?
>
> Where did this need for acceleration come from? Why is moving so quickly so important?
>
> What will happen on their end if you can't meet this schedule? What are the stakes for them around the new deadline?
>
> Why this deadline in particular? Why today rather than tomorrow, a week rather than two, or two weeks rather than a month?
>
> Does every element of the deal need to be done within that time? Or are there certain elements that are more urgent than others?

These questions are not easy to ask because your ego will make you believe that you are upsetting or insulting the other party. But asking them is vital to the success of the negotiation. On the one hand, if the other side has a legitimate reason for the time pressure, you need to understand their expectations and their decision process if you fail to meet their timeline. Once you understand that, you can work with them to find a way to meet their needs, or respectfully let them know that schedule doesn't work for you.

On the other hand, if the other side doesn't want to share the reason for their sudden time pressure, it is likely that they don't have a justification and are just trying to bully you. In this case, giving in will hurt you twice—not only will you lose out now, you'll also let them know using time against you works, which means they'll do it again in the future. So, don't do it.

Being mindful doesn't mean that you can't call out dishonest or manipulative behaviors. In fact, calling out those tactics is exactly what the C4 step will help you be able to do.

One final reminder: remember, negotiation usually happens over multiple meetings, scheduled out over weeks or even months. It's incredibly rare to go from the first proposal to a closed deal in just one day (no matter what was portrayed on *Mad Men*). You shouldn't expect your first proposal to be accepted without any pushback—or believe you must accept their first proposal without raising objections or making counteroffers.

Do one-day deals happen occasionally? Sure. But if the other side does accept your proposal without pushback, it's probably not the home run you think it is. More likely, you didn't ask for enough and settled for less than they'd have been willing to give. Same thing if you accept their proposal right away—they probably would have been willing to give more, you just didn't ask for it.

In the next chapter, we'll talk about how to approach subsequent meetings, counteroffers, and objections—without losing sight of C4U™ or letting your ego take control.

Alexis Checks In With Mia

"I lost it," Alexis cried. "I completely, totally lost it." She was sitting in her car after work that day, calling Mia before starting her drive home.

"Wait, what? You lost the deal?" asked Mia.

"No, no," replied Alexis, "I lost control and I forgot about C4U™."

"So, you didn't lose the deal?" inquired Mia.

"No, but I lost my head. I was upset and didn't follow your guidance," said Alexis.

"Tell me what happened," said Mia gently.

"Well, I was totally aware of all the fear I felt in the moment. He was aggressive and interrupting me, and I felt my stress level rising and my breathing getting shallow."

"Then what happened?" said Mia

"He stood up with his face less than a foot away from mine, and he was insisting that I give him another proposal. The walls closed on me and I didn't know what to do."

"You said you didn't lose the deal," said Mia. "How did you close the meeting?"

"He said he wasn't prepared to accept a three-year deal and still wanted the best price. At that point, I was able to share with him that nobody in the market has such a deal, and that he won't be able to get a similar deal elsewhere. I even questioned him about the reason why he didn't want to commit for three years. That struck me as weird, as it was the first time he'd ever mentioned it," said Alexis.

"Okay, then what?" asked Mia.

"I proposed another two-month extension at the current price to give us an opportunity to create a deal that would be mutually acceptable for both parties," said Alexis.

"That's good, Alexis, isn't it?" said Mia.

"Yeah, I guess it is, now that I think about it," said Alexis. "And the best part was, I got him to agree to meet with me next week and be fully open about what he needs."

"Alexis, that is amazing!" said Mia. "But you started this call totally upset, saying you lost it. Why is that?"

"Because I completely forgot about C4U™! And I almost screwed up the whole deal—it was really only luck that let me salvage things."

"So, you're feeling judgmental toward yourself for not being able to use C4U™ the whole time, is that right?"

"Yes," mumbled Alexis. "I thought I had it, but it just flew right out of my head as soon as Lucas started talking."

"Do you remember when I shared with you that C4U™ needed practice and that you won't be able to master it overnight?" asked Mia.

"Yes, but…"

"There is no but, Alexis," said Mia. "You were aware of your feelings and you were curious about them, so you at least started C4U™. Then, when the tension

was intolerable, it sounds like you were unable to connect with self-compassion. That's okay."

"But I was supposed to…" started Alexis.

"You weren't supposed to **do** anything," stated Mia. "You did your best, and you had enough mindfulness and clarity to move the negotiation forward rather than letting it fall apart. This is very good, Alexis. Now tell me, what did you learn from this morning?"

"Other than the fact that I wasn't in perfect control, and have a lot more practicing to do?"

"Yes, other than that," said Mia, smiling.

"Well…I think one thing I realized was that until the point where I didn't follow the C4U™ model, I was pretty good about being aware of how I felt."

"That's a great observation, Alexis. Anything else?"

"Um…well, this kind of falls under making different choices. Once I got past my ego and made the choice to ask Lucas about his reason why we couldn't agree to three years, I felt in control of my stress and my emotions, even if he didn't really answer my question. When I made the choice of not being intimidated by him, I honestly felt like I could stand up for myself—for the first time in maybe ever!"

"Good!" said Mia. "That's exactly the kind of breakthrough I was hoping you'd have today. You have more work to do around self-compassion, but you'll get it in time. Then you'll be ready to not let your ego bring self-judgment or criticize you, like it did this morning, C4U™ will flow better."

"Thank you," said Alexis. "Next time, I'll be ready for it."

"That's the spirit," said Mia. "I'm curious, how did Jorge take this news?"

"Oh, him," said Alexis. "He didn't like it one bit, let me tell you. At least I got to tell him privately instead of in front of everyone."

"Did he yell?"

"No…I think he wanted to, but I managed to get out in front of it this time. I chose to present my solution as a positive, that there's a good chance of salvaging the account now. He didn't like the two more months at current terms thing, but he did like the idea of reverting to list price after that if we can't come up with anything. I think that more than anything was what kept him from blowing up."

"*That sounds promising,*" said Mia.

"*I think so, too,*" said Alexis. "*But he made it clear that this was my bed and I have to lie in it. I think he's going to wait and hope I screw it up so he can say he told me so.*"

"*And maybe he is. But you've got a secret weapon!*" said Mia.

"*I know! And I'm hoping it will help me get a grumpy skeptic to work with me for the next two months—and pay more than he wants to.*"

"*It will,*" said Mia. "*Take it one meeting at a time. Now when you come over tomorrow, we'll talk about how to find out what Lucas and his company really value—and how to give it to them without giving up everything YOU value.*"

"*That sounds great! I'll see you then.*"

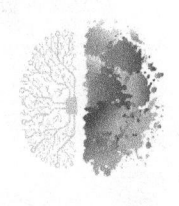

Chapter 8
NAVIGATING THE SLOPES

*"The best move you can make in negotiation is to think of an incentive
the other person hasn't even thought of —and then meet it."*
—Eli Broad

Alexis Asks Questions

One week later.

*"Lucas, how are you this morning?" Alexis asked as she opened the conference
room door.*

*"Eh, I'm not bad," Lucas said. "I gotta tell you, I was surprised my boss bit on
your strategy. I thought for sure Marco was gonna tell me to walk."*

*"You know, I felt the same way about my boss," said Alexis. "I half expected Jorge
to fire me for doing an end run around him, not to mention costing him two more
months at your current discount."*

*"Heh," laughed Lucas. "Well, either we're both onto something or we're both
screwed, am I right?"*

*"Here's hoping it's the first one," said Alexis, giving him a nervous smile. "Now,
I was reflecting on what you said last time we've met, and I wanted to ask you a
question."*

Lucas frowned. "I suppose. What is it?"

"What does this deal mean for you?"

"Excuse me?"

Alexis straightened her shoulders. "If this contract gets renewed. Or doesn't. Or does, but not at great terms. What happens for you in those cases? It feels like there is a lot at stake."

Lucas blinked. "Well, um, as you probably know, my organization needs your company's products, but we don't have—"

"I'm sorry," Alexis interjected. "I don't mean what happens for your company. I mean, what happens for you, personally? What does Lucas Olivera get out of this contract?"

"I...you really want to know that?"

"I do!" said Alexis firmly. "I know we got off on the wrong foot—two wrong feet, even—but I really do want this deal to work out well for both of us—not just me!"

Lucas looked at Alexis for a very long moment. Then he seemed to deflate, slumping down heavily in the chair and staring at the tabletop. Alexis waited, barely daring to breathe.

"I've been at HMG for twenty-two years, did you know that?" he finally said.

"I think so, yes," breathed Alexis. "That's an impressive track record, especially these days."

Lucas barked a laugh. "Yes, you'd think that, wouldn't you? But do you know when my last promotion was?"

"Um...I don't, actually," said Alexis, mentally kicking herself for not learning that in her research about Lucas and his company.

"Eight years ago," said Lucas. "And since then, I've seen half a dozen younger buyers who've only been there a year or two promoted past me—most of whom then promptly leave the organization for an even better position elsewhere. How do you think that feels?"

Alexis found herself nodding sympathetically. "That sounds awful. It must be frustrating to feel like you're standing still and everyone's passing you when you're working as hard as you can."

"Exactly!" exclaimed Lucas. "You described it perfectly, that's exactly how I feel. And no one here seems to care. I'm pretty sure my boss—who's closer to your age than mine, by the way—sees me as a dinosaur."

"That's terrible," said Alexis. "I'm so sorry." Then a thought flashed into her head. "Lucas, this deal..." she began slowly, "is this your last chance for a promotion? Or even to keep your job?"

Lucas's head snapped up, his eyes meeting hers for the first time in several minutes. "That's not what I said! Did I ever say that? When did I say that?"

I shouldn't have said that! *thought Alexis.* But wait—he's not angry at ME. Maybe I don't have to be afraid? Maybe that's just my ego talking...

"You didn't," she said gently. "It was just a guess. But I did ask what this deal meant to you, and you mentioned missing promotions and your boss thinking you're a fossil, so I put two and two together. Was I totally wrong?"

Lucas sighed. "No, you weren't. I made a deal with my boss. If I keep this contract in favorable terms, I get the next promotion that comes up. If I don't, I stop asking for one—forever."

Alexis's eyebrows went up. "Wow, that's...that's some deal. So, you've got a lot riding on this."

"Yeah, no two ways about it. So, like I said, I need a deal I can work with here. None of this five percent below your previous proposal crap."

"You mentioned last time that you weren't prepared to commit for three years," said Alexis, resisting the urge to react to his insult. "That was completely new to me. Why does HMG have that position now?"

Lucas was quiet for a moment. Alexis bit her lip, thinking hard. I think my ego wants me to talk and fill the silence. But I'm in control, not it.

"Okay," sighed Lucas. "You might not know it yet, but we have acquired Mid-West Care, another group of hospitals. The deal is official as of this morning, but we aren't announcing it for another two weeks."

"Congratulations," said Alexis automatically, wondering what this might mean.

"Thank you. The challenge is that MWC has a lot of different lab equipment than we do. We have to uniformize our diagnostic lab technology with theirs, as well as the reagent kits we both use for blood testing, so every site can operate from

the same platform. A three-year contract on the reagents we're currently buying from you won't work, because we might not even be using that equipment anymore in eighteen months."

Alexis' eyebrows went up again. "That's…not at all what I was expecting to hear," she said. *"You're looking to change your equipment? That's a completely different negotiation."*

"In what way," asked Lucas. *"You're going to make me a lopsided proposal anyway, aren't you?"*

Alexis bit back a sharp reply. Ego, I know that's you! *she thought.* Now stop that! I don't need to argue with him just for the sake of arguing.

"No, that's not what I meant," she said. *"I meant that I walked in here today thinking we were just talking about renewing the contract on reagent kits. Now you're talking about buying new capital equipment for diagnostic labs. There's a lot more value in this deal that we haven't explored yet—value for both sides!"*

Lucas gave her a skeptical look. "Uh…really? That's not what your company is known for… creating mutual value."

Alexis nodded. I can feel my heart speeding up. Breathe, Alexis. You've got this.

"I know it's not," she said. *"But maybe it could be…and either way, I think the best deal here will be the one you want as much as we do."*

Lucas nodded slowly. "Alright. Let's say we can put together a deal like that. What else do you need?"

"Well, like I said in our last meeting, I need us to be completely open with each other. You've already started doing that by telling me about your new equipment needs, so let's follow that path. Tell me about the capital equipment you want for your diagnostic labs."

Lucas spent the next several minutes explaining what the new labs needed. Alexis took notes, occasionally asking a clarifying question. Once Lucas was finished, he asked for a quick break to make a call and refill his coffee. Alexis used the time to gather her thoughts.

Wow, I'm so glad I didn't skip this step! *she thought.* Getting all this information from him felt tough going into it, but I can see so much more value for the contract now. Just listening to Lucas these last few minutes was so much better than letting my ego take over and run my mouth!

When Lucas returned, Alexis offered to summarize what she'd gotten from his descriptions.

"If I heard you correctly, you are looking to buy diagnostic equipment worth approximately $1 million in aggregate, as well as universal connectivity systems for that equipment so they can all talk to each other. You're also looking to have that equipment installed and set up in your HMG facilities, including as many of the new MWC labs as possible, within the next 12 months. You'd like a 24/7 long-term service agreement for that equipment, with a local service engineer who lives within 100 miles of HMG headquarters. You plan on purchasing the current reagent kits you get from us, ideally at the same price as the current contract, until all the new equipment is purchased and installed, at which point you will start buying new-generation kits. And you would like a stipulation that any HMG site that isn't able to upgrade its diagnostic equipment through this capital purchase can continue purchasing the current reagent kits for the length of the contract. Oh, and of course, you want all of that at our best prices. Did I get everything?"

Lucas nodded. "That sounds about right…plus, I'll need you to help me save face with my boss."

Alexis felt her stress rising as she prepared to ask the next question. "Okay, so which of those elements do you want most?"

"What do you mean, most? We need everything, I told you!" said Lucas.

"Well, let's assume we can't give you all of them right now, because let's be real, we can't. If you had to pick the top ones, the most important elements, what would they be?"

"You're killing me here." Lucas gave Alexis a highly skeptical look. "How exactly is this creating value for my company if it's taking out most of the things we need?"

Alexis consciously stepped on her ego's urge to roll over and give in. "Because in order to give you the most value, I need to know what you value the most! I need you to tell me what's an absolute deal-breaker to lose, what's important but not vital, and what's just nice to have."

"Fine, okay," said Lucas. "Getting diagnostic equipment that will work seamlessly with what we already have is a must. I just double-checked with my boss, and we definitely do want to go with your company for that equipment, as we already have a couple pieces of yours in HMG headquarters. And the connectivity platform is just as important. Now that we're working with so many MWC locations, it's vital that all our sites be connected together on the same platform—doctors need to be able to read results from anywhere, outpatients can have their lab tests done at any site, and we'll save money by reducing redundancies. And getting your best price on both of those is also a top priority."

"Makes sense," said Alexis, taking more notes. "What's after that?"

"The next thing would probably be the reagent contracts, ideally at the same price we're paying now. We need a contract that will allow us to use the current reagent kits until we acquire the new equipment and the new generation's reagent kits afterward, without interrupting the purchasing and shipping of the kits or changing the price around in the middle of things. Along with that, we'll need a contract without a volume commitment for the current reagent kits for the sites that don't get a new piece of diagnostic equipment. These contracts will ensure a smooth transition to the new generation without breaking the bank. And I should point out these are about as important as the capital equipment needs. We're not going anywhere without these contracts—or rather, we're not staying here unless they're here, too."

"Got it," said Alexis. "What else?"

"We would like to have the 24/7 long-term service agreement for the new equipment with a service engineer that lives locally, within 100 miles of HMG. With the volume of tests we are doing this year with the virus crisis, we can't afford to have equipment down for a while."

Alexis bit back a grin, remembering something Jonathan once told her about how to pay attention to the way people are talking. Lucas just said he would like the reagent contracts **ideally** at the same price, and that he **would like to have** a 24/7 service contract. Both of those words mean it's not really a priority. I wonder if...

"Alexis? What is going on? You seem far away," asked Lucas.

"Oh! I'm sorry, I was just processing what you shared with me," replied Alexis. "You mentioned a 24/7 service contract. Those are very expensive. What is your concern in asking for a 24/7 contract and having a local service engineer?"

"We want to make sure that if something happens, that the equipment is not down for too long. So, a 24/7 service contract with a local service person makes sense," said Lucas.

That confirms Lucas expressing the service contract as a "like to have." It doesn't sound like a must for him, *thought Alexis.* "If we can find another way other than a 24/7 service contract and guarantee a level of uptime for the equipment, would that work for you?"

"I guess," scoffed Lucas. "I don't see how it would be possible to guarantee that, but if you have a solution I haven't thought of, I'll take a look at it."

"Okay," said Alexis. "Thank you for sharing what you did. This is very helpful." Lucas nodded. "So, what's next?"

"Now, I'm going to take this information back to my boss and my company, and we're going to design a proposal that gives you as much as possible of the things you value most. Let's meet again in a week to discuss that proposal," concluded Alexis.

"Okay, I think I'll believe that kind of proposal when I see it, but we're already doing this, so let's talk in a week."

○——————————○

When You Think You Know Everything About the Other Side

As you now know, negotiation is about creating value for both sides. You can't create value if you don't specifically understand the other side's needs.

Why bother asking the other side what they need? You have been doing business with the same buyer or the same salesperson for the last five years, after all. You know what they want—or at least you think you do.

And yet, how often do you find yourself in a situation where the other side rejects your proposal—one you think is giving them everything they want? Especially when you're offering them a lot of money?

Remember, negotiation isn't about money. It's easy to believe that all the other side wants is money, but money alone doesn't create value for both parties. There is a lot more than just money that matters in negotiation: saving face, proving yourself, being recognized, avoiding losing the deal or being judged, etc. If it's true for you, it is also valid for them.

To really create value for the other side, you need to understand the other side's constraints, pain points, drivers, and motivation—especially when they say things like "you're too expensive" and "we need better pricing." When you hear statements like that, your job is to probe around and find out what's behind them. Maybe they really do need more money, but likely there are other factors at play as well.

If you do try to write a proposal or counteroffer without that knowledge, you risk upsetting the other side, you don't build trust, and ultimately you drag out the negotiation process much longer (and may even destroy it).

Meanwhile, your ego wants you to believe that you have all the relevant information already. (It also creates a paradox for you: even if you think you know what the other side wants, your ego will tell you not to offer it to them. Why? Because your ego wants you to win, which means they have to lose.)

Let's take a moment (C1) to be curious (C2) around this concept of discovering and understanding your counterpart's real needs, motivations, and pain points.

1. What kind of emotions do you feel as you dive into this topic?
2. What challenges do you associate with discovering and understanding their world?
3. What happened the last time you thought you knew exactly what the other side wanted? Did you actually know? What was the outcome? How did you feel about what happened?
4. Does the idea of understanding the other side make you feel vulnerable? Why?

This can be a tough scenario to confront mindfully. After all, you've likely been trained not to think about the other side's needs and to focus on your own. You might feel some resistance as you explore this topic. You might want to stop being curious. You might feel angry at me for even bringing it up! That's okay. That's just your ego telling you you'd be better off not being curious. By now you know how to bring compassion (C3) to that moment. Remember there are no right or wrong answers or feelings here.

The More You Know About the Other Side, the Easier It Is To Create Value For Both of You.

I like to think of this process of understanding the other side like surveying the terrain ahead of you on the mountain before you start the next part of the climb. The more you know about what's ahead, the more successfully you can navigate your way to the summit.

Let's explore other ways (C4) of surveying the terrain before you make a proposal or counteroffer.

1. What if, by being curious about the other side's drivers, motivations, and pain points, you can demonstrate to yourself and your boss that you are a skilled negotiator?
2. What if by doing that you could discover elements you didn't know about before, that will help create more value and build more trust?
3. What if you can increase your credibility with your internal team by providing information about the other side that they didn't know before?
4. What if understanding the other side will help you close the deal faster?

Being curious about the other side's world is not a sign of weakness. It's quite the opposite, actually. You are demonstrating to the other side that you are not like everybody else they've ever negotiated with--that you actually care about them, not just yourself. And caring about your counterpart doesn't mean that you will give them everything they want. It means you are genuinely interested in delivering a mutually beneficial proposal, not one that only helps your side.

When you attune to the other person in the moment, you bypass your ego and choose to negotiate in a more authentic and empathic way.

Let's be clear here: if you're going to do this, you need to walk the talk. Don't just say you want to understand the other side and then keep talking yourself. That's what your ego wants you to do.

Ask all the open-ended questions you wrote down during your preparation and *actually listen to their answers*. The majority of us don't actually listen to the response when we ask a question. We are preparing the next question in our heads or focusing on what we will say next. Don't let your ego pull you away from truly listening to the other person.

It may take some time for the other side to fully open up to you. People are hesitant to share when they feel vulnerable or when there is a lack of trust at the table. If the other side is reluctant to share or doesn't provide a real answer to a question about a pain point or need, don't let your ego ignore the lack of response and move you on to the next question. If you don't get your question answered, ask again from a different angle. If you're asking the questions, it's because you need the answers.

You can also propose to trade information (your objective or priorities) for their information (priorities, pain points). This practice often helps to build trust.

If you try many different ways of asking your questions without getting anything in return, it might be the time to call the other side out on it. You might say "It looks like you are not prepared to share anything with me today. It will be really difficult for me to go back to my internal team and design a proposal that is valuable for you if you don't share information with me. Is there anything you'd like me to know that you haven't shared so far?" This last effort may encourage them to share—but even if it doesn't, you'll still have beaten your ego and done your best to understand them.

When the Other Side Wants Everything…and More

There are three ways the other side can communicate that they want everything you can give them—and probably a lot that you can't.

The first level is during the conversation, where they casually bring up all their demands. (This is the situation Alexis set up when she arranged to ask Lucas all of her information-gathering questions.)

The second level is when they come to you with their proposal listing all their specific requirements. (This is what Lucas likely would have done if he'd been the one proposing first.)

The third level is the most emotionally challenging to receive: when they come in with an extreme and inflexible proposal right from the get-go. (This is what Jorge told Alexis to do in her first meeting with Lucas!)

In each of these situations, your ego will react. It might tell you that you have to agree with everything they ask for. It might tell you to dismiss their demands as ridiculous. If they're aggressive, it might even tell you to fight back because it's already in fight-or-flight mode.

One thing is for sure: if your ego is in control, you are stressed, and you likely do not feel you have a clear path forward. The challenge here is that the conversation revolves around them exclusively, without any space for your needs.

Let's pause here (C1) and be curious (C2) of what is brewing inside of you:

1. What emotion comes up when the other side demands so much?
2. What experiences in your past does this remind you of? When else have you faced unreasonable demands in your life? How did you feel then?
3. Do you find yourself wanting to give in to the demands or push back against them?

Don't let your inner critic be in charge here. Take a moment to bring compassion (C3). You won't be able to connect with other ways of being if you don't have compassion for yourself, because self-compassion allows you to have compassion for your counterpart. You know they're in their ego, but you also know what that feels like, so it's a short step to bring your compassion over to them. When you meet their ego with compassion, it loses the power to trigger your ego, which means that you can stop the chain reaction of egos before it starts.

Now, let's bring C4 to explore what else you can be doing:

1. What if you can pivot and manage the situation without damaging the relationship?
2. What if you can shift power back toward you and regain control?
3. What if the threat is an empty shell designed to pressure you?
4. What if you can show them a path that gets them the value they want without taking value from you?

Your Job is Not to Give Them Everything They Want. Your Job as a Negotiator is to Find Out What They Really Need.

First, stay present and listen attentively. Once they are done sharing their proposal, take a moment to repeat back to them what you heard to make sure you understood their proposal correctly. If you can, repeat it using the same wording and language they used, as they might have chosen less assertive words (would like, hopefully) that can help you identify their priorities.

Then, ask if you've missed anything. This forces your brain to pause and consider instead of jumping in with a response right away. It also builds trust, as it shows the other side that you were really listening to them.

Next, ask them clarifying questions about their proposal:

Can you walk me through how you came up with this proposal?

What information did you base this proposal on?

Who owns these demands: you, your boss, your CFO, your CPO?

What specifically will this proposal do to meet your business goals?

How do these terms compare to those you are requesting from other vendors?

These questions are beneficial for any proposal coming your way, especially when it's a proposal with extreme demands. Ask more questions if you feel you didn't get enough information. These questions help them slow down their brain and use their frontal lobe in a way that offsets their ego.

The next step is to share with the other side that you can't give them everything they want (refer to the section on delivering bad news in chapter 6). If they ask for something specific you can't agree with (company policy, guiding principles, etc.), you need to let them know right up front to set their expectations. Otherwise, your job now is to understand where the other side has flexibility in what they're asking for. To do this, you'll need to get some clarity on their priorities by asking some questions:

Of the three elements you named, which one is most important to you?

What part of the proposal will have the most crucial impact on your business?

Why are these particular elements more/most important to you?

If you had to rank these needs in order of importance, what would that look like?

Which of the items you listed do you need right away, and which could potentially happen later?

Be warned: They will *always* try to convince you that everything they asked for is top priority. (Of course, they will—they want you to give them all of it!) But you both know that isn't true—even when they legitimately want everything they're asking for, they will always want a few things most.

Note: If they say they want a specific thing but can't explain why or how they came up with it, then it is likely not their top priority. If I'm negotiating something crucial to my business, I won't have any problems being specific and sharing the data that led to my position.

This process is vital to the success of the negotiation! You can't go back to your team to start crafting a counteroffer until you understand their highest priorities. Keep asking and following up on these questions. If you pay attention to the answers and keep probing to get additional details, you'll be able to see through any nonsense and learn what they really need. Be compassionate ("if I were in your shoes, I'd probably ask for everything you're asking for, too") but stand your ground ("as I mentioned, I won't be able to give you everything, so I need to understand what's most important to you").

If the other side refuses to be flexible on their demands (i.e., they will not name priorities and keep demanding everything), you have a couple of options.

You could simply tell them all of *your* demands in response and ask them if that works on their end. You could present a hypothetical scenario, saying *if you could* give them all of their demands, here's what you'd need in exchange. Or you could call out their lack of flexibility:

> "It sounds like you are not prepared to share your highest priorities today, and as I explained earlier, I can't go back to my internal team with all of these demands. I propose we stop the meeting and resume our conversation at another time."

This will be a big shock for the other side, as you are not speaking from your ego, and you are in control of your emotions *and* the situation. Calling out behaviors or emotions is a potent mindfulness tool, and most people (and their egos) are not prepared to deal with it.

One last insight about priorities: You might face a situation where the other side's priorities change over time. This could be legitimate, or it could be a tactic from the other side to get more than what you are prepared to offer. Regardless of the reason, you need to call it out.

> "I thought you mentioned earlier that your priorities were A, B, and C, and now it seems that D, E, and F are your priorities. Help me understand the reasons and motivations behind this change. What do these new priorities mean for your company? When did the shift happen, and when were you planning on sharing the new priorities with me?"

This is a great mindful approach as it demonstrate that you are fully present. You will be amazed by how powerful this approach is. You are telling the other person that you actively listen to them and that you see what they are doing. If their priorities changed during the course of the negotiation, it shouldn't be difficult for the other side to provide an explanation. If the change was merely to get more from you, it will quickly become obvious.

When You're Doing All the Talking

One of the biggest temptations in a negotiation meeting is to fill every moment with words. Your ego loves this plan, because when it's talking it feels like it's in control. Silence is like kryptonite for your ego because it makes the ego feel like it's losing control of the situation. But the reality is that by talking nonstop you actually hurt your side's position.

If you let your fears control you at this moment, you will talk just to fill the silence, and likely either provoke a rejection from the other side or give them a concession they haven't even asked for yet. Don't fall for this trap, even if the other side is quiet for a long time.

This is particularly important right after you deliver a proposal or a counteroffer. In this moment, the other side is quiet. They haven't actually said anything yet. Which means your ego is going to try to fill the silence. Don't let it! It will talk you down from your own proposal and turn a good deal into a bad one, just because it's afraid the silence means it's about to get rejected.

Knowing when to stop talking is even more important once the other side has rejected or objected to your offer.

A couple of chapters ago, I mentioned persuasion as one of the tactics the ego likes to use to try and retake power from the other side. Trying to persuade the other side to agree with you is an easy pit to fall into, because usually it sounds like what you're supposed to be doing anyway: presenting the features and benefits of your offer to the other side so they understand how great it is.

Problem is, you've already said everything you're saying now. The other side already knows what you're offering them, and they've already told you they don't like it. You just don't want to admit it—or rather, your ego doesn't.

When you try to persuade, you may think you're building trust with the other side. In reality, you're doing the opposite: you're telling the other side you think you know better than them, you're smarter than them, and your needs are more important than theirs. You also tend to sound condescending, like you think the other side is too stupid to negotiate for themselves.

Put yourself in their shoes for a moment. Imagine someone asks you to do something you don't want to do. Then when you say no, they attempt to persuade you to change your mind, repeating themselves over and over. How would you react? Would you actually change your mind after the other person repeats the same argument seven times? Or would you feel beaten down, ignored, disrespected, and talked down to?

This is how the other side feels when your ego convinces you to try to persuade them. And because you're listening to your ego, you won't notice the signs that they're feeling that way. You'll just notice that they keep saying no, and so you'll keep repeating yourself louder and louder until the other side's ego reacts to yours.

Here's an easy way to tell if you're trying to persuade: if you're the one doing all the talking.

A negotiation is an interchange. Both your side and the other side need to contribute. But egos don't like silence, so if the other side shuts up, your ego will try to make you keep talking—usually by persuasion.

Let's pause here (C1) and be curious (C2) about persuasion:

1. What are you trying to demonstrate or achieve by doing all the talking?
2. What emotion is coming up that makes you want to use persuasion?
3. Is persuasion really getting you closer to your objective? How can you be sure?
4. What are you afraid will happen if you stop talking or if persuasion fails?

Not stopping at the first obvious answer is critical here. This is probably the most challenging situation to be curious about as you might not know on the surface exactly why you are behaving this way. You might need more than one session of being curious (C2) before you start uncovering the real drivers behind your desire to do all the talking.

Your Ego Isn't Aware When Persuasion Doesn't Work. It Thinks Failure Means You Just Didn't Try Hard Enough Yet.

Connect with self-compassion (C3). You might have just realized that you're not as good negotiator as you thought. That's okay! Like I said, persuasion is sneaky. Your ego associates successful persuasion with your self-worth. Don't push back on whatever comes up here. You're not alone; everyone deals with this problem.

The good news is, persuasion has a short shelf life or window of opportunity. Generally, after 10-15 minutes, persuasion becomes inefficient—at that point it's clear even to the most stubborn ego that the other side won't be persuaded. The bad news is, even within that short time, persuasion can trigger a lot of ego on the other side and do a lot of damage to the negotiation.

Let's explore other ways that can work outside of persuasion (C4). The only way to take control back from our ego is to distance yourself mindfully from the situation and become an observer. Ask yourself:

1. Are you doing all the talking? Is it working?
2. What if you could be in control and successful without persuading?
3. What if you didn't have to prove anything to yourself or to the other side?
4. What if your offer might not be the best one for both sides, and persuading the other side to accept it would actually hurt you as well as them?
5. What if your confidence was based on gathering information and using that information to create the best proposal for the other side, rather than trying to prove yourself with persuasion?

What's the opposite of persuading? Asking questions! As you learned in the last chapter, you can't create value for the other side if you don't know their motivation and their pain points. The best way to create value for the other person is to be curious about their reality.

Remember surveying the terrain! If you haven't asked them already, go back to the list of questions you compiled during the preparation stage and start asking them one at a time. If you didn't write any questions in advance or you've already asked them, switch your brain into discovery mode and come up with questions about the objections your counterpart raised.

And once you stop talking, don't let your ego convince you to start again. When you ask a question, the other person might take several seconds before answering. That's okay! Be mindful and don't be afraid of silence even if you don't feel comfortable being silent. Your ego and wants you to believe that you need to talk to diffuse tension. But you are in control of the conversation because you are asking questions. Keep that control by being mindful of the silence and letting the other person answer in their own time. Often, that pause is just the other side considering their answer—it's not about you at all.

If the other person is avoiding your questions or providing vague answers, you may need to keep asking the same questions again and again or rephrase them to get clear answers. Your ego doesn't like that, as it is afraid of upsetting the other side and will tell you to move on to the next question. Listen to the other person, not your ego.

Pay close attention to the other side's emotions as you do this. If they are getting upset, you are likely getting close to something they don't want to share or feel they can't share. When that happens, remember that their emotional response is not your fault (C3). You don't own their reaction; you are simply being curious as a way to find the best possible solution. Try sharing information or asking encouraging questions instead of responding with emotion yourself (C4).

Navigating the lower slopes of your negotiation mountain will be challenging, but as you survey the terrain and choose each new path mindfully, you'll find your way and start making progress towards the summit. But don't get complacent! As you climb higher, the mountain will start to rumble under your feet…as your counterpart starts to raise serious objections. In the next chapter, we'll talk about how to mindfully quiet these rumblings without causing an avalanche.

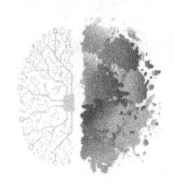

Chapter 9

WHEN YOU FEEL THE MOUNTAIN RUMBLING

"Treat objections as requests for further information."
Brian Tracy

Alexis Stands Up to Jorge

"So, let me get this straight," said Jorge. "You've been talking with Lucas for a month now. You've brought him all the things we need to keep this contract favorable for us. And now you're coming back to me saying not only is he not willing to commit to volume for ordering reagent kits, but that we should give him our best pricing on them anyway?" He threw up his hands. "What could possibly have given you the idea that I'd sign off on that? Oh wait, I know, you want to create value, that's it. Well, I liked that idea at first, but I was thinking that maybe, just maybe, you'd actually create some value for us!"

Alexis cringed as Jorge's fist slammed down on his desk with the final words. Breathing faster, hands shaky—yep, definitely feeling scared, ego definitely going into protection mode, *she thought, barely registering that those thoughts came almost automatically this time.*

"Jorge, that's not what I said—"

"Oh, I'm sorry," Jorge spoke over her, his voice dripping sarcasm. *"Did I misunderstand how my newest protégé wants to give away the farm? How do you think this company runs, Alexis? By offering the best pricing without getting volume commitment? You know, you're really making me wonder why I invited a know-it-all girl like you into the leadership development program in the first place."*

Something snapped inside Alexis. Suddenly she found herself on her feet, leaning over Jorge's desk to meet his eyes from just a few inches away.

"Stop it," she said, her voice snapping like a whip. *"You've been riding roughshod over me for months now because that's all you know how to do and because I've let you. Well, that ends today."*

Jorge's mouth dropped open in surprise—and so did Alexis's! Holy cow! I didn't know I could do that! Was that a C4 choice? *she thought, all in a rush. Then, before she could think any further, she found herself speaking again.*

"I get that you don't love how I'm learning to negotiate, Jorge, and I can appreciate that. But your way isn't the only way, and if you'd actually bother to listen to me all the way through, you'd know that I'm not trying to give away the farm or even give Lucas everything he wants. What I'm trying to do is give him as much as we can of what his priorities are—so that he gives us as much as he can of what we want! That's why I'm meeting with you this morning—to tell you what he's asked for and what I've managed to get from him in return! Do you think we could actually talk about that? Or do you just want to belittle me and ridicule me and bully me until I quit and drop the whole mess in your lap?"

With that, she plopped back down in her chair, breathing heavily.

Jorge remained frozen in place for several seconds, apparently too surprised to move. Alexis felt her stomach begin falling into her shoes as she waited. I made that choice, I made that choice, I made that choice, *she repeated in her head, understanding for the first time what Mia had meant when she talked about the sheer courage of choosing something different than her ego wanted: her ego's desire to judge herself for being too harsh or aggressive.*

At length, Jorge unfroze and sat back down, looking off into space. *"I didn't think you had any backbone at all,"* he mused. *"I thought you were a mouse, like all the other mice who come through here—a mouse I have to teach how to be a tiger."*

Alexis found herself grinning. "To be fair, I probably was a mouse until a couple minutes ago," she said. "I don't, um…usually do that."

"No, you don't," said Jorge. "But I'm glad to know you can do it—and I bet you are, too."

"I'll let you know for sure when my legs stop shaking," Alexis said.

Jorge threw his head back and laughed. "A tiger after all! A tiger in mouse clothing, yes?"

"Sure," said Alexis. "If that makes you happy, sure. Now, can we try this again? And are you going to listen and help me this time?"

Jorge was still laughing. "Alright, why not? Maybe this old tiger can learn something new today."

Alexis gave a sigh of relief. And maybe this mouse learned something today, too!

"Alright," she said. "So, originally, it seems that their interest in signing the new contract was only to avoid paying list price."

"I knew it!" interrupted Jorge.

"Please, let me finish," said Alexis. "They didn't want to commit for three years, either. But now I'm finally ready to tell you why, because they officially announced it this morning."

"Announced what?" Jorge looked interested in spite of himself.

"HMG has acquired another group of hospitals. Lucas knew about this when we started talking, and it's been the basis of our negotiation since, but we had to wait for the official announcement to talk about it outside the conference room.

"Anyway, within the next couple of years, they need to uniformize their lab equipment and reagents across their current locations and these new hospitals. So, you're right, they don't want to commit to volume for the next contract—and believe me, Lucas and I went back and forth over that for a week—but they DO want to buy all the diagnostic equipment and a top-end connectivity platform from us as part of the renewal. So, really, we're talking about a much bigger contract than before—one where the volume commitment on reagent kits isn't as big a deal for us."

Jorge stared. "I had no idea about any of this."

"Neither did I, until I started asking Lucas what he and HMG really needed."

"Okay, so we've got a sizeable equipment and software purchase. Now we're talking! What else did he say they needed?"

I knew he would like that, *thought Alexis, smiling at her boss.* Mia was totally right about what's important to him!

"They want our best pricing on all the equipment, of course—there was a little wiggle room there, but not much. They want to be able to transition from their current generation of reagent kits to the newest one when the platform is installed but have any site that doesn't get the new equipment to be able to keep ordering the current kits. That's why the volume commitment has to be variable for them."

Jorge opened his mouth, but Alexis raised a hand and kept going. "They also want a long-term 24/7 service agreement with a service engineer that lives locally. They are concerned about losing operation time if the equipment goes down. Lucas also mentioned that, ideally, he didn't want to pay more than the current contract price for reagent kits. But he's been less emphatic when talking about both of those elements, so I think there's more flexibility there."

Jorge was nodding slowly. "Yes, that makes sense. Have you talked much about those last two points with him yet?"

"Not much yet," said Alexis. "We've largely been hammering out details on the big stuff so far—the pricing on the diagnostic equipment, which software package works best for their needs, the installation and setup schedule, that kind of thing. I've got notes on all of that here."

"Okay, good," said Jorge. "Tell me about them."

"Well, the biggest objections Lucas had were the pricing of the diagnostic equipment and the installation schedule. Fortunately, we worked out pricing pretty easily, but we hit a major snag around getting all the pieces installed and connected within 12 months."

"What was that?"

"It was something you told me the other week, actually. You were talking about how we have a manufacturing backlog of nearly 12 months on our end, and I realized that would make a 12-month schedule pretty much impossible for new diagnostic equipment."

"You're right," stated Jorge. "But even with that, couldn't we push for exactly 12 months? Or 15 at the most?"

"I thought about that, but there are so many different locations that the logistics of getting everything installed and connected will likely take an additional six months, minimum. So, even if we start with the first piece as soon as it's ready, it will still be at least 18 months before everything's online, and closer to 24 is more likely."

"Ouch," said Jorge. "That's not good. What did you have to give him to make up for that?"

Alexis breathed in deeply, remembering that she controlled her fear, not the other way around.

"First of all, I gave him the same explanation I just gave you—that as much as we'd like to meet a 12-month schedule, it just wasn't possible without going back on our word to other clients who've been waiting longer than HMG."

"And he accepted that?" Jorge looked highly doubtful.

"Eventually, after I showed him the relevant documentation," Alexis continued. "It took a while, and I think he had to eat some crow with his boss, but he eventually got the okay to aim for an 18-month schedule instead, with flex time up to 24 months if needed. In return, I offered to cover the full transportation costs for all the setup work, which turned out to be an extra fee HMG was very glad not to have to pay."

Jorge raised his eyebrows. "But that's nothing for us. We have a whole budget line for that kind of transportation."

"We do, but HMG doesn't," said Alexis. "Something else I learned by asking Lucas what would be valuable for him, and something that gives them a lot without taking much away on our end."

"So, they agreed to the extended schedule without taking it out of the equipment price?" Jorge sounded astonished.

"Pretty much," said Alexis. "We'd already dickered quite a bit on the equipment, so it didn't feel right to drag it back into the negotiation when an easier solution was staring us in the face."

"I see," said Jorge. "And the reagent contract…you said they couldn't commit to volume because…?"

"Because they don't know exactly what the volume will be yet, mostly," said Alexis. "And they probably won't know for sure for three years, once everything has been set up and running for a year or more and it's clear which locations will be getting the new generation kits and which won't. So, not having to commit to a specific volume on *a three-year contract is super important to them. I actually used that to get a higher equipment price than they initially wanted."*

"Alexis, this is twice you've impressed me in one meeting. I really thought you were going to give Lucas the farm just to keep him on as a client. Thank you for explaining all these details to me—even the ones I didn't want to look at right away."

Alexis beamed. *Jorge was thanking her?* Not in a million years did I ever see that coming! *she thought.*

"Now, since you clearly have the big stuff well in hand, let's talk about some of these smaller things where there might be more flexibility," he said. "What ideas do you have on those?"

And he's asking me for ideas? Knock me over with a feather! *thought Alexis.*

"Well, one idea I had was to offer a firm price on reagent kits for the length of the contract."

"Could work," said Jorge. "But it would have to be for the new generation kits only. As our volume decreases with the current kits, our manufacturing costs will go up. We need to protect our margins."

"That makes sense," answered Alexis, making a note. "So, I could offer firm pricing on the new generation ones, but insist on a price increase for the current kits in return for no volume commitment. How does that sound?"

"Now you're thinking like a tiger, Alexis," said Jorge. "Lead with that when you get to that element—and don't let Lucas push back too hard. Mutual value or not, the reagent kits are a big part of this, and I don't want to lose money on them. What about the service engineer question?"

"I'm not as sure where to start with that one," said Alexis, firmly stepping on her ego's aversion to admitting ignorance. "Maybe a tiger I know might have some thoughts?"

Jorge laughed. *"He just might. Here's what jumps out at me…"*

When Alexis left Jorge's office half an hour later, Kamal was so startled by the smile on her face that he dropped his coffee mug on the floor.

○——————○

When the Other Side Raises Objections

There are few things more frightening than being partway up a mountain and hearing the ground far above you start to rumble. Avalanches and mountainside earthquakes kill climbers and hikers every year. When you hear the mountain rumbling, you have three options: abandon the climb and turn back, try to reach the summit and get back down again as fast as possible, or proceed with caution and prepare to adapt to quickly changing circumstances.

Nothing in a negotiation process will physically hurt you. Getting an objection from the other side isn't like having a rock fall on your head! But there's a pretty close parallel between how to handle a rumbling mountain and how to handle objections during a negotiation.

Your ego hates objections mainly because they point out things we didn't do well. Remember, being told it's wrong or it made a mistake is a nuclear-level threat to the ego. And that goes double for finding out someone isn't happy with it! The ego must be 100% right and completely welcome all of the time, or else it throws a fit. Your ego wants you to think that objections are attacks on you, your offer, and your company.

When the other side objects, they're likely in their ego. So, rather than being calm and collected, they're defensive, angry, scared, contemptuous, or frustrated. And then, when *their* ego starts throwing its weight around, it triggers *your* ego to want to defend itself or run away. More often than not, this turns into a vicious cycle with each side's emotional ego provoking the other party's in turn until both sides are entirely drowning in emotion. Your survival instincts kick in, and you want to either leave the room, hope that you can address the objection quickly and move on, or simply give in.

Let's take a moment here (C1) to be curious (C2) about what is coming up:

1. What comes up for you when you receive objections from the other side?
2. What emotions are you experiencing in these moments?
3. What is your little voice telling you at this time?
4. How do you deal with objections in other parts of your life?

If you feel like you failed, are scared of being judged by your boss or feel any other emotions, don't forget to bring compassion (C3). It's okay to feel these things. There's nothing wrong with them, or with you for sensing them. Feeling emotions when you get objections is entirely natural. Don't beat yourself up. Realize that it's the ego's desire to defend itself.

Please consider that the objections aren't personal—they're about your proposal, *not about you*. Does that help you to feel different about it? Be curious (C2) about it.

Now that you have slowed down your brain and your ego is not in control anymore, let's explore other courageous choices (C4) around *not* doing what your ego wants.

1. What if objections were a source of information instead of being an attack?
2. What if objections were a sign that you did all the talking earlier in a previous meeting and missed something about the other side?
3. What if you could take control back without being defensive?
4. What if an objection could lead to a new opportunity to be creative and find a solution both sides like?

Hearing the Other Person's Rumblings About Your Proposal Is the Best Thing That Can Happen to You!

The fact is that objections are a source of information the same way emotions are a source of information.

If the other side raises concerns about your proposal, that means they are interested in it! If they weren't, they wouldn't be talking to you about it at all. The good news is that at this point, emotions are still pretty mild. There may be some frustration or irritation, but usually the first objections the other side raises aren't explosively emotional. Yet. Clearly, *something* about your latest proposal or counterproposal is triggering fear or frustration on their part. They're trying to tell you what it is and why it's a problem so that you can fix it

If you get curious and try to understand their point of view, they will tell you what you need to do to create more value for them.

Now that you understand that they aren't personal, let's embrace objections. Did you notice there is an "s" at the of objections? Very likely, the other side will have more than one objection. Your ego isn't going to like that! It wants to take control and get power back by fixing every objection as it comes up. It's so scared of objections that it can't even handle hearing more than one at a time.

But you're not your ego! You actually want to hear all the objections up front, because maybe you can fix or solve or remove more than one at a time. So instead of doing what your ego wants you to do and dive into fixing the first one right away, you might want to be curious and ask, "What other concerns or objections do you have?" Keep asking that until your counterpart has listed them all. When the other side is done with their objections, mindfully recap everything you heard.

Then, do the same thing you did with their demands in the last chapter and ask them what their priorities are. The intent here for you is to let them know that you can't be flexible on everything (like in the previous section, when you couldn't give them everything they wanted). Some of their objections will be bigger and more important than others. You want to focus your time handling the ones that matter the most for the other side. Otherwise, you might run out of flexibility before you tackle the most concerning objections.

You will notice at this point that you haven't actually started to handle the objections yet. By now, your ego is screaming to get going. But before you start, you need to ask one more question. Here it is:

"If I can handle your most concerning objections, will you commit to moving forward with this deal?"

You ask this question now because you don't want to handle a bunch of difficult objections now, only to find that there are more to handle later. (Note that this is one of the rare times when a yes/no question is appropriate, rather than an open-ended one.) Your ego will not want to ask this question, because it will feel like it's opening you up for rejection. But the C4 choice is to ask it anyway.

If the answer is yes, then your job is to understand the objections you need to address as clearly as possible, so you can take them back to your team and find the best solutions you can offer.

If the answer is no, your next question needs to be, "What else is preventing you from moving forward?" What they say next will be gold for you: either it will reveal information you don't yet have (that they may not have planned to share with you), or it will reveal their true intentions toward this negotiation (that might well be that they don't want to go through with it). Either way, you will get valuable info to bring back to your team. Listen carefully to what they say and how they say it. Don't let your ego react.

When the Other Side Threatens to Walk Away

One of the biggest triggers for your ego is when someone threatens to walk away from the negotiation entirely. This is a very aggressive behavior that tells you how much the other side is in its ego. Oftentimes, this tactic is used to gain power and scare you at the same time. Other times it's a desperate move from a counterpart who feels they have no other options. The bottom line is that negotiators use this tactic because they are not getting what they want, and they feel threats and ultimatums are the only way to make it happen.

At this point, it's not a negotiation anymore. It is a situation where the other side is trying to impose their will to get what they want—without giving anything in return. They know you can give them the thing they're asking for (if they knew you couldn't, they wouldn't ask for it), and they're choosing to push you to give it to them for free or lose the deal entirely.

This is the one thing no-one wants to hear. As soon as your ego hears that they'll walk away if you don't give them what they want, it automatically goes into fight-or-flight mode. Fear spikes, judgment rises, and you don't know what to do next other than give in. In all the stressful moments of negotiation, this one might be the one where it's hardest to think clearly.

So it's even more important than usual to take a moment (C1) to be curious (C2) about what is coming up when you heard this threat:

1. What is coming up as you hear the possibility of them walking away? (You will likely experience different emotions. Take your time to explore them all).

2. How does this demonstration of power toward you impact your professional and personal senses of status?

3. Where else in your life have people threatened to walk away from you? How do those experiences inform your response in this situation?

As you go through these questions and peel back one layer at a time, you might experience different levels of emotions, from surface-level irritation to deep sadness. Don't dwell on judging or criticizing yourself. Bring compassion (C3) and be gentle toward yourself. The emotions that come up around people leaving us are some of the toughest we'll ever face. It's okay to feel confronted, shaken, or threatened by them. But even they can't control you unless you let them.

Now, let's explore alternative choices (C4) to respond to this demand without letting your ego take charge:

1. What if the other side is playing this card because they feel they don't have power?

2. What if threatening to walk away is an empty threat you can uncover?

3. What if you can retake control of the situation without giving in to fear?

4. What if their demand is a wake-up call for you to do a better job of listening to them and giving them what they need?

Breathe. Your job now is to be the observer who sees the other side without judgment. They most likely aren't making this demand because they actually want out of the deal—if that were the case, they'd just walk away without making any demands. That means they probably still need you. They just need something you haven't been willing to give them yet. So now you get to use your mindfulness skills to figure out what that thing is, why they need it, whether you can actually give it to them, and what they're willing to give in return.

Yes, this means you're going back into information-gathering mode. Here are some helpful questions to ask in response to this demand.

Questions about the proposal or demand itself:

What is their total demand in dollars or % of business?

Who is asking for these requests (them or their boss)?

Are they asking the same terms from all the vendors they're talking to?

What are they trying to accomplish with this demand? What is driving it?

What have you missed that's vitally important to them?

If you could give them what they're asking for, what would it be worth adding to the deal on their end?

Questions about their behavior:

Why do they feel the need to threaten you to get what they want?

What was the trigger that made them change your approach and threaten to walk away?

After all the work they've done with you over the last weeks or months, why do they feel the need to threaten a walkout now?

What's changed for them since the last meeting that makes walking away an option?

Questions about what could happen next:

If you can't meet this demand and they walk away from the deal, what will happen to them/their company?

What if, by forcing you to agree to this demand, the deal becomes unworkable later and your company decides to scrap it in six months or a year (or simply can't maintain the demanded terms)?

Have they considered what impact this demand might have on your working relationship with them in the long term?

The purpose of these questions is to retake control of the conversation—both from your ego and theirs. You need to understand the reasons, the drivers, and the pain points behind their demand. The more you gather information, the more power you have to make a counterproposal that will keep them at the table, and the less your ego will want to take over.

Most likely, if you are mindful and ask these questions, it will take the other people off guard and help them open up to sharing more information with you. Be curious and ask them about what you have missed. You might also want to recap what you've heard so far and how your proposal does in fact give their priorities (as far as you know).

This is not the time to persuade. If you genuinely missed something, you need to be willing to own your mistake and work with them to find a solution. But it's also not the time to give away the farm just to keep them at the table. If they ask you to create additional value for them, you need to find a way to create value for you as well.

If the other side gets upset with your questions and goes silent or restates their demand, let them know you can't go back to your team without understanding where they're coming from and what they're trying to achieve.

The goal of this process isn't just to keep them from walking away, it's to help them give you the information you need to propose a deal that works for them. Mindfully asking these questions, listening with compassion, and showing them, you care about meeting their needs will nearly always lead to a calmer counterpart and a successful deal—even if you really can't give them the thing they want.

As a final note on this section, remember to never give in to threats. Take 24 hours to think before you agree to anything. You don't want to reward bullying or aggressive behavior.

When You Need Additional Flexibility From Your Boss

You might think that the time between external meetings should be a break from being mindful. After all, you're not in the heat of the moment anymore. There's no other side to deal with, and the pressure of the negotiation has eased for a few days. But as relaxing as it can be to be out of the meeting space for a while, do you really think it's *you* that's telling you to stop being mindful? As tempting as it might be to forget about mindfulness until the next meeting, don't fall for that ego trap.

Besides, now that you know what the other side needs from you, there's a good chance you're headed for another negotiation: the one where you ask your boss for more flexibility than they want to give you.

In this scenario, you know that you've reached your limit—you can't offer the other side any more flexibility (on price, volume, time, availability, etc.) by yourself. But the other side has made it clear that limit isn't flexible enough for them. You've already gathered all the information you could, and you've already used C4 to try to find creative options, but there are still some things they need that you can't authorize. You need your boss's permission to offer those things.

This negotiation can be even more challenging and emotional than the one you're having with your counterpart, especially if your boss likes to listen to their ego (and let's be honest, a lot of bosses do!).

For starters, just having this meeting means you have to deliver bad news—either you delivered a proposal that got rejected, or the other side gave a proposal that wasn't workable for you. It's easy to feel like a failure—or at least like your boss will see you as one—when that bad news has to be your starting point. Fear, self-judgment, and other negative emotions will likely come up as well.

Not only that, but your boss is already pre-framed to come to this meeting thinking you're giving away the farm and that your request isn't trustworthy. When I was a VP of Sales, I rarely felt I could trust my reps when they asked for flexibility. Why not? Because in my experience, whatever limit I set for them was exactly what they'd just offered the other side. If I gave them a higher limit, they'd start offering that amount instead—without asking for more value in return. As far as I could see, the more flexibility I gave them, the more they used it without creating additional value for our company. This is the perspective your boss will most likely bring to this meeting: that you're simply trying to make your own job easier without getting anything extra in return.

So, as you're preparing to meet with your boss, take a moment to find awareness within yourself (C1) and get clarity around what is coming up for you and why (C2).

1. Do you feel accountable for the negotiation needing additional flexibility, like it's your fault? If so, why?

2. What is coming up as you consider your role in this situation?

3. Are you sure you've done absolutely everything you can on your own? How do you know?

4. Which action is a bigger source of anxiety: Your negotiation counterpart pushing you beyond your limit? The possibility of your boss' ego being in control?

5. How do you think asking for additional flexibility will impact your reputation as a negotiator?

6. From an observer's perspective, why is this situation happening? Is one side or the other more responsible? What can you learn from what's happening here?

7. When else in your life or career have you needed to ask for additional flexibility? What happened then? What was the outcome? How did you feel about it?

It is easy to allow your ego to defend you and prevent you from being in touch with the real reasons why you are in this situation. The essential element here is to keep asking yourself why for each answer, especially if you feel yourself becoming defensive.

As you are curious about these things, bring compassion toward yourself (C3). You might be afraid of being judged, looking incompetent, or being blamed for a difficult situation that wasn't entirely your fault. These are natural things to fear! *Bring compassion even if you feel it's not your fault.*

Regardless of what emotions you're feeling now, bringing your ego to your boss won't help—and will most likely work against you. So, let's explore some different choices (C4):

1. What if you can demonstrate to your boss that you have a plan, a solution, and that you are in control?

2. What if by owning your responsibility (even partial responsibility) for the need for extra flexibility, you could help your boss understand the needs of the negotiation better?

3. What if you can show additional value that will make the extra flexibility worth giving?

4. What if you could present this scenario as a learning experience for you—and explain what you've learned and how it will help this or future negotiations?

5. What if by being mindful and not getting emotional, you can help your boss take back control of their emotions get away from their ego?

This is one of those scenarios when your being mindful and keeping control away from your ego will help the other side do the same thing—even if they don't know it. By meeting your boss's ego with your own mindfulness, you can steer the discussion away from emotional reaction and towards rational responses on both sides. You may have to stand up to your boss a bit, like Alexis did in our narrative, but if you do it mindfully, their ego won't have any ground to stand on.

Believe it or not, your boss doesn't want to be completely inflexible. But they also don't want to feel like they have to do your job for you. If they are going to give you flexibility, they need to know that you'll get them value in return. They want to know that you have a plan, not just that you're asking for more leeway because you've run out of other options or don't know what else to do.

Being Proactive and Demonstrating That You Have a Plan to Deliver Additional Value to Your Organization Will Go a Long Way to Display Your Leadership as a Negotiator.

Don't let fear, judgment, and other negative emotions guide your behavior. Mindfully prepare for this meeting with your boss. Review your counterpart's priorities, constraints, and pain points. Come prepared with a plan that will deliver additional value for both organizations.

If you realize that you don't have enough information about their priorities and pain points to explain why the flexibility is needed, don't let your ego control you. Stop the self-judgment and your inner critic. Propose an action plan to your boss to find out what you are missing.

Nobody (other than your ego maybe) expects you to be a great negotiator without practice. Your boss will understand that you are learning—as long as you show them that you actually are!

Finally, make sure that your boss supports your next move with your counterpart. Whatever flexibility they give you, make sure you're both clear on what it is and what you'll be asking for in return.

By staying mindful even as the other side starts to get emotional, you will anchor the negotiation in a calm presence and allow the other side's emotion to drain away. Their ego deflates, their frustration fades, and they start to connect with you constructively. Before you know it, you've resolved their objections, moved on toward the next counterproposal, and are making progress toward the mountaintop again.

Before we move on, let's take a moment to celebrate (C5)! Handling rumblings and objections is *not* easy. Stress and fears kick in, your ego wants to grab the wheel, and you can feel the emotional chain reaction happening as each party triggers the other person. You followed the process of mindfulness, you asked questions and used creativity to explore different solutions, and you brought the meeting back to a calm collected resolution. And it wasn't that scary—or even if it was, you knew exactly how to handle those fears. Congratulate yourself for being able to stay present and mindful during this situation—and get ready to have an excellent report for your boss on how you turned the other side's objections into a path forward.

Chapter 10
WHEN THE VOLCANO ERUPTS

"No one can make you feel inferior without your consent."
—Eleanor Roosevelt

Alexis Stands Her Ground

"Hi, Lucas!" Alexis called cheerfully as she approached the conference room door two weeks later. She'd just gotten off the phone with Mia and was feeling pretty good about the progress of the negotiation. Yes, she and Lucas had had a lot of points to debate. The last meeting with Lucas hasn't been easy as Lucas brought up several new objections to the proposal. But all in all, she felt the new contract terms were shaping up to be pretty good for both sides—and maybe more importantly, she'd been able to rely on C4U™ to stay calm and mindful during the more stressful moments.

Lucas was holding the door open for her, and as Alexis reached him, she could see he didn't look happy.

"Look, I'm sorry about this," he muttered in response to her quizzical look. "It wasn't my idea."

"What wasn't…oh, I see," said Alexis, as she noticed the third person waiting inside the conference room. He wore an expensive suit, mirror-bright shoes, and an expression of impatience.

"Alexis, this is my boss, Marco," said Lucas, *following Alexis in and closing the door.*

"Good morning, Marco," said Alexis, *extending her hand.* *"It's a pleasure to meet you."*

Marco shook her hand wordlessly, then spoke curtly to Lucas. *"Let's get this started. Tell her the situation."*

Lucas nodded and turned to Alexis. *"Marco has decided to sit in on today's meeting. He's...hopeful that his presence will help get us closer to a deal today."*

"That's not what I said," Marco snapped. *"What I said was that today's meeting is the last one. Either we come to terms on this contract today, or we're not renewing it at all. Get me?"*

Alexis nodded, her heart speeding up, but her mind stayed surprisingly clear. *"Well, Lucas and I were getting pretty close to terms we could both agree on, but we do have two more weeks before the deadline. Can I ask why you don't feel the need to use the full amount of time we agreed on?"*

"I have my reasons," said Marco coldly. *"Lucas, give her the proposal we discussed yesterday."*

Lucas gestured for the three of them to sit down at the conference table. As he sat, he pulled a page out of a folder and began to read from it.

Your all-digital diagnostic laboratory equipment with universal connectivity platform, priced at $945,000

Installation and setup of equipment and platform within 18-24 months

No volume commitment and no price increase on the current generation reagent kits

All-inclusive service contract with uptime guaranteed

Three-year contract term with firm pricing for the new generation reagent kits and equipment service

"So, tell me," said Marco. *"Are you going to take those terms, or are we done here?"*

Alexis took a deep breath, remembering she didn't have to pick one of those two options—she could choose to create a third one.

"Well, I don't think we're done here—after all, the meetings just started," she said. *"And if we need to come to terms today, we can. But I have to be clear: they won't be the terms Lucas just read off. There are three points, in particular, he already knows aren't workable for us: the diagnostic equipment price has to be $995,000 we can't honor the last contract price on the current reagent kits, and we need a five-year contract, not three. Lucas and I agreed on these terms at our last meeting. I don't understand why you disagree with them today."*

"Because they're BS terms, and you know it!" Marco exploded, leaping to his feet. *"You know darn well the proposed terms give us the short end of the stick. You know how much they'll cost us. And somehow, you've got Lucas here wound around your pretty little finger so tightly that he's just taking whatever you offer and liking it! Well, I'm not going to sit here and let you screw us over, do you hear me? Either you take these terms, or we're done!"*

Alexis could feel her ego boiling up in the back of her mind, ready to freeze her in place or keep her mouth stuck shut in the face of her counterpart's boss screaming in her face. But instead of letting the fear boil over, she began gently rubbing the back of her neck with one hand. This is supposed to trigger me into giving in, *she thought.* And it's definitely still a trigger. But this isn't my dad yelling at me, or even Jorge or Lucas yelling at me. I don't need to be afraid of them anymore—and I don't need to be afraid of this blowhard triggering me or trashing the deal. I can choose not to be terrified!

In that moment, Alexis suddenly felt a sense of deep clarity. Everything in the room—the still-shouting Marco, Lucas staring at his notes, the hum of the fluorescent lights, the smell of the coffee on the sideboard—all snapped into a focus so sharp it was almost digital.

This must be what Mia told me about, *she thought,* when everything slows down sometimes. It's…wow! I'm not afraid at all, just calm and ready. I can feel my fear and ego wanting to come out, but it's like they don't even matter. I think I've just gotten the hang of this!

"Are you even listening to me?!" Marco raged, *noticing Alexis appeared to be staring into space.* "You have one job to do, and it's to accept the terms I just laid out! Are you going to—"

Alexis stood up. Startled, Marco fell silent as the young woman met his eyes.

"No, Marco, I'm not," Alexis said coolly. "What I've offered is absolutely the best we can do—and it's a much better deal than you're going to get by walking away and starting over with our competition. Lucas knows it. I know it. And I think you know it, too. I hear you—they're not the terms your organization has had for the last six years, and I can see how difficult it is to let go of those terms. But this contract is different from the last few ones, as you are planning to buy capital equipment and use the new generation's reagent kits, among other things."

Marco sputtered, unsure of how to take this.

"It sounds like there are a lot of emotions around this contract, maybe because it's so different," Alexis went on. "But I'm sure Lucas has already told you why the terms need to be what they are. So, what's really behind your anger here?"

Marco narrowed his eyes at her. "Just who do you think you're playing with? You've been in this business what, a year? Two?"

A-ha, thought Alexis. "Two and a half, actually…but why does that matter to you? I'm still helping you get the best deal you can, aren't I?"

"Bah!" spat Marco. "Lucas has been doing this for over twenty years. You're still in kindergarten!"

Alexis nodded. "So, what I'm hearing is that you're having trouble trusting my judgment on these terms because I'm relatively new to this industry, is that right?"

"Yes, that's exactly right," said Marco. "You don't know the realities of this business yet—if you did, you'd be giving us much better terms."

"I see," said Alexis. "You know, when I look at this from your perspective, that actually makes sense."

"It does?" said Marco, stunned.

"It does?" echoed Lucas.

"Sure," said Alexis. "You're absolutely right, I'm the new kid in the room. I'm still learning how to negotiate. So, I completely understand why you'd hesitate to trust me."

"You…you do?" Marco sounded even more confused.

"Of course I do," Alexis continued. "And I want to apologize if I made you feel like I was trying to steamroll you or pull any wool over your eyes to make up for my lack of experience. That's not where I'm coming from at all, and if that's the impression you got, I'm really sorry."

"Well, I didn't say that…" said Marco. "Lucas certainly tells me you've been professional and polite, but…"

"But how can I possibly know more than he does?"

"Something like that, yeah," grumbled Marco. His anger seemed to be fading, but he was still a long way from happy.

"Is there anything else bothering you about this?" Alexis asked.

"Well…now that you mention it, yeah. I know who your boss is, and I know his style—browbeating the other side into submission. I also know Lucas is too good to fall for that. So, what I want to know is how you got my veteran salesman to accept these terms!"

"Actually," interjected Lucas, "can I answer that one?"

Marco waved a hand. "Well, someone needs to!"

"Marco, when I first started meeting with Alexis, I thought the same thing you're thinking right now—either this rookie girl is going to try to intimidate me or manipulate me into rolling over. And I started our negotiation even more skeptical than you are. But Alexis didn't do either of those things. She asked me what we needed. And then she did her best to give it to us in return for what her company needed, and she was completely honest with me about what they could and couldn't do."

"Are you really saying you think these BS terms are the best ones we can get? From them or from anyone?"

"I am," said Lucas.

"And you'll stake your promotion on that?" Marco clearly wasn't done playing hardball.

"I will," stated Lucas calmly. Alexis flashed him a grateful look, mouthing "thank you" over Marco's head. Lucas smiled back.

Marco paused for a moment, then pointed one finger at Alexis. "Alright, fine. Lucas clearly believes what you say. But I'm not convinced yet. I want to talk to your boss. Right now. If he's behind you on this, then fine. But if not, then we're done here."

Oh, no, thought Alexis, her heart sinking. Jorge's gotten a lot better recently, but even after our great meeting two weeks ago, he's never fully gotten on board with creating as much value for the other side as for ours. The only way I got him to fully approve this contract was to extend it from three to five years. Okay, it's okay, I can still choose something other than panic.

"My boss knows everything that I know," she said. "I've discussed all of the terms with him. I don't think he'd say anything different than I have."

"Yes, but of course you'd say that," said Marco. "Lucas, look up Jorge Sanchez's number. I'm going to call him right now."

Lucas supplied the number, giving Alexis an apologetic look as Marco dialed the conference room's phone.

"Hello? Yes, I want to talk to Jorge Sanchez." There was a pause. "Jorge? It's Marco, from Health Mountain Group. I'm standing here with someone who says you're their boss." Pause. "Alexis something."

Alexis breathed deeply in and out as Marco described the situation to Jorge. I've made my choices, she thought. Whatever happens, I'll be ready for it.

"Yes, that's exactly what I'm saying," said Marco into the phone. "I don't believe she's coming clean with me. I think your company can give us the terms we want, and she's trying to screw us out of them by holding this deal over our heads."

I'm holding it over your head? Alexis thought idly. You're the one threatening to walk out...

"What do you mean, what do I want you to do about it?" Marco continued. "I want you to tell her to give us the terms we want and stop jerking us around! Look, we all know how the newbies can get, hot to prove themselves, but you and I have been around long enough to know what works, and this doesn't...I'm sorry, what was that?"

Alexis's breath caught in her throat. It's okay, it's just my ego. She made herself start taking deep breaths again.

"I...are you telling me you support this proposal?" Marco sounded like he'd been punched in the stomach. "That you're behind this beginner and her terms?" Pause. "What do you mean, value?" Pause. "Well, I mean...I guess we're getting some value from it, but that's not the point!" Pause. "I see." Pause. "And you're sure that's the best your company can do? Absolutely sure?" Pause. "I understand. I'll...go talk to Alexis again now. Goodbye."

Was that what I think it just was? Alexis's eyes were wide, she hardly believed what Marco's side of the conversation seemed to be telling her.

"What did he say?" asked Lucas. "It sounded like—"

"Yes, yes, he supported what Alexis said about the terms on those three points. And he had quite a bit to say about you, young lady," said Marco. "Apparently, you've got his full authority and support for this contract."

"I'm glad to hear it," said Alexis. Especially since I didn't know I had it myself until just now! "So, what do you think?"

Marco sighed. "I think…I think I need to hear your final proposal, the one you and Lucas were going to review today."

Alexis exchanged a small smile with Lucas. "Very well, here's what my company proposes:

> **Digital diagnostic laboratory equipment with universal connectivity platform, priced at**
> **$995,000**
> **Installation and setup of equipment and platform within 18-24 months**
> **Price increase but no volume commitment on the current generation reagent kits.**
> **All-inclusive service contract with uptime guaranteed**
> **Five-year contract term for the new generation reagent kits and equipment service, with firm pricing for the first three years**

"Does that sound right to you, Lucas?" she finished.

"It lines up with what I expected you to bring me after our last meeting, yes," said Lucas.

"Well, I have to run it by our finance and legal departments," said Marco. "But if they give me the green light, then I'll sign it."

"Great!" said Alexis. "I'll schedule another meeting next week so we can all sign it together."

Marco just nodded.

"Oh, and one more thing," said Alexis as she gathered up her bag. "I heard you mention Lucas's promotion. Will we be celebrating that next week as well?"

Marco looked pained but nodded again. "Yes, we will. Lucas, good work."

"I owe you," Lucas whispered as he walked Alexis out. *"I don't know if he would have gone ahead with the promotion if you hadn't said that!"*

"I thought as much," said Alexis, grinning. *"But you really do deserve it after how hard you worked with me on this, so I figured I'd stick my oar in just a bit."*

"Well, I'm grateful. Next time you need a favor, call me."

"I'll do that," said Alexis. And here I thought he was a jerk at first, *she thought.* I think C4U helped him as much as it helped me.

When Emotions Explode Across the Table

Rumblings on the mountain are a clear warning to tread carefully. But a volcanic eruption, an avalanche, or an earthquake are much more dangerous. You can't take time to consider the best way to respond—you need to be ready to move immediately!

The same is true in a negotiation. When the other side is yelling at you, bullying you, getting aggressive, or otherwise letting their emotions control them, you don't have time to make a plan. You need to be ready to respond right away! In moments of explosive emotion, the difference between success and failure can be measured in seconds.

The problem with these moments is that we may not see them coming until it's too late. Then suddenly, we're getting yelled at, insulted, or even walked out on, and we have no idea why. So, the second you realize the other side is erupting, you've got to get a handle your ego *right then and there.*

Why? Because your ego will perceive the other side's emotional outburst as an immediate threat. A person shouting at you isn't too different from a bear roaring at you! Your ego will process that input and immediately tell you to fight back, run away, or surrender.

An eruption across the table means the other side is overwhelmed by emotion—it's literally pouring out of them like lava. Their fight-or-flight instinct, driven by their ego, has taken over. They aren't thinking clearly and won't hear or acknowledge your point of view. In their mind, they are fighting for survival and will do almost anything to win—even hurt you.

A volcanic eruption is a lot of boiling lava being forced through a tiny space in the earth's crust by immense pressure. You might think of it like a fire hose, except with liquid rock instead of water. So, how successful do you think it would be to stand in front of the eruption and try to force all that magma back into the mountain?

Not very.

So, the absolute *worst* thing you can do when your counterpart's emotion is being forced out of them at explosive speeds by their ego…is to try to rationalize the situation and get them to calm down. *No one* wants to be told to calm down when they're emotionally overwhelmed. Logic and rationality are counterproductive at this point. They'll just lead to an even bigger explosion.

Persuasion is almost as bad. Defending, overselling, repeating the advantages of your proposal, blaming someone else, or rejecting responsibility will just set the other side off even more.

Clearly you don't just want to give in, either! If you have to make a concession, don't ever give in under threat. Your ego wants you to stop the volcano by giving in. If you do that, you will reward aggressive and bullying behavior.

And, of course, it never works to fight lava with lava. Meeting their emotional outburst with an emotional outburst of your own will just make the whole situation worse. Remember that the buildup of pressure inside the volcano forces the magma out through the weakest point in the rock. If you get emotional and start projecting your fears onto the other side, you just became the weakest point in the negotiation—and the full force of the other side's eruption will fall right on you. But when you are mindful, you can divert the lava flow and help it begin to cool down.

There's Already One Person in This Meeting Who Can't Think Clearly Right Now. Don't Make It Two

Negotiation techniques and tactics won't work—they won't even occur to you—if you're in your emotions the same way the other side is in theirs. The only way out is to manage your ego right away when an eruption is happening.

So, as the other side starts to blow up, and your fears and defenses begin to rise, *immediately* take a deep breath and focus on the moment (C1), so you can start looking inward instead of outward. Allow time to slow down so you can process what's happening and respond appropriately. And before your ego gets a chance to start screaming at you to *just do something already*, start being curious (C2) about what's coming up for you.

1. What is coming up for you at this moment? *Likely, you will experience multiple emotions here. Just take your time to explore each of them. Name what you feel, it helps you detach from it and observe it.*
2. What does this volcanic eruption do to your level of confidence and your ability to close the deal and maintain the relationship?
3. What other personal situations does this volcanic eruption remind you of? What happened in those situations? What emotions come up when you remember them?
4. What is your ego telling you to do or say in this moment?

Since eruptions get right in your face with the other side's emotions, your curiosity will likely reveal aggressive feelings like pain, rage, powerlessness, and shame. Make sure to meet these emotions with compassion (C3) before your ego can start to run with them.

Remember, whatever the other side is saying or doing right now, *it isn't personal*. Even if it's happening because of a mistake you made, you're not the source of their reaction. It's theirs. You don't own their emotional response, and you aren't responsible for it.

You haven't created this emotional mess. Really, you haven't. Even if what they're reacting to is your bad proposal or your failure to listen to them. This eruption is their ego taking control of them, pure and simple. You didn't have the reaction coming to you, and you aren't doomed because of it. Don't let your ego interrupt and make you believe that you now have to please the other person or avoid upsetting them more by giving in. This emotional eruption doesn't control you, and neither do the emotions coming up for you.

I like to think of this process as becoming a seismologist—a scientist whose job it is to understand volcanic eruptions and why they happen. Once you detach yourself emotionally from the situation, you can observe it as separate from your own experience and start learning about what's really going on—both across the table and in your own inner world. Instead of thinking, "he's mad at me!" you can observe that the other side's face is flushed and his voice is raised. Instead of thinking, "I'm scared!" you can note that your shoulders are tight, and your breathing is shallow.

It will help here to take your attention off the other side for a moment. Look around the room or out the window. Remember that your life is much bigger than this individual erupting in anger or fear.

Take a deep breath to slow down your heart rate. Focusing on your breath for two to three seconds will help activate your frontal lobe and mute your survival instinct.

Rub your hands together or massage your neck to nurture your body and help you stay mindful. By giving yourself a bit of physical comfort, you are connecting with positive, caring energy that will help in being self-compassionate (C3).

Now, recognize what's just happened. By bringing compassion to the moment, you have completely shut down your ego and reminded yourself that you aren't under its control. So, now you can choose a different path forward that isn't the emotional one your little voice wants you to take (C4). Instead, connect with the fact that the other side isn't aware that their ego is in full control of them—and that because you *are* aware of that, you're the only one who can help them take that control back.

1. What if everything happening is not about you personally?
2. What is this situation revealing about the kind of person you are? The kind of person they are?
3. What if this eruption was the strongest signal that the other party needs help dealing with their own ego?
4. What if you can stay calm and present, take control back, and still have a chance of closing the deal?

More than anywhere else in the negotiation process, being mindful in the face of an eruption is critical to creating a positive outcome.

Being mindful when the other side is lost in emotion doesn't just help you; it also helps *them*. Your calm courage gives them an anchor of rationality to hold onto, so the flood of emotion doesn't sweep them away. Ultimately, your mindfulness can save the negotiation.

By Being Mindful and Compassionate, You Will Help the Other Person Regain Their Composure.

Erupting people want to be seen and heard. So, **listen to them.** Your job here is to fully understand where they are coming from a neutral, empathetic perspective. Do this calmly and without judgment, letting them say what they need to tell you. Maintain eye contact and breathe deeply. You may want to put your hands together in front of your heart with your palms facing each other and your fingers pointing toward the ceiling. This is a sign of calm and confidence.

Now that the other person is a bit calmer, you need to **address the concern behind the emotional outburst.**

It is likely something very personal—fear, anger, or shame. Maybe they're afraid of losing face or seeming incompetent or not getting their bonus this year. Perhaps they're angry because they feel insulted, disrespected, or like you aren't listening to them. Maybe they're ashamed because they thought they could get a better deal, or they aren't as prepared as they should have been.

Your job is to understand what that feeling is and why it's coming up by asking about it directly. Ask as many follow-ups as you need to. You have to get to the bottom of their emotions before you can even think of moving forward. That will help cool off the lava and potentially prevent further eruptions.

The task here is to direct the other side's emotion into a positive channel, where instead of merely exploding at you, they're explaining to you *what* triggered their upset and *why* they feel the way they do. This helps them feel heard and acknowledged and shows them you care about their side of things. Make sure you're actively listening when they talk, though! Don't use these questions to lead into persuasion or to dismiss their concerns, or even to plan what you're going to say next (all ego behaviors).

Another great mindful approach is to **mirror what you just heard.**

Repeat back to them what you are hearing using the same words they used. The objective here is understanding. You are not judging their reaction, and you are not labeling them in a specific box, you are just playing it back the same way they communicated to make sure they feel fully heard, and you completely understand their issue. In my experience, it is one of the most powerful tools to help the other side understand that I'm there for them and hear them. This might sound like:

> What I'm hearing is... is that correct?
> It sounds like... am I hearing you correctly?
> I want to be clear on what you just said, the issue is that...?

Finally, connect with your self-compassion and **empathize with them.** Put yourself in their shoes and acknowledge their pain and their emotions. You might say:

> I'm sorry that I've missed what was important for you. I apologize for putting you in an awkward position with your peers.
> I'm sorry; it was not my intention to create this tension or this emotional situation.
> I apologize if I wasn't clear in my communication with you. It wasn't my intent to hold back onto that information and to make look bad in the process.
> You can even share how you would feel if you were in their shoes:
> I can totally understand where you're coming from. I'd feel exactly the same way if I were you.

This is a fantastic empathy moment to help the other person feel like they are not alone in their world, that someone else could feel the same way they are. You can't empathize with them if you are not mindful. This is one of the most potent mindful approaches to build trust.

Now that the other side is a bit more relaxed, you might be tempted to rush back into the negotiation. Don't! Trying to get things "back on track" put the other side back into their emotions. Tt tells them you don't *really* care about them; you're just listening long enough to get what you want.

Calming the eruption will take as long as it takes. Let it.

You Can't Focus On the Business Issue Until the Lava Has Cooled Down.

Your ego will hammer at you to move forward and not ask any additional questions. Don't listen. Mindfully, continue asking the other side questions until they've said everything they need to say:

What else is there?

Anything else you want to share or that is still bothering or upsetting you?

Listen to what they are saying and use the same process as above and ask the same questions again until they are done. You'll be able to tell they're done when their body releases tension. They may slump down in their chair, put their head in their hands, or release a long breath. Being in their ego takes a lot of energy, so once they can let go of it, they'll be tired!

Now That the Emotional Bubble Has Deflated, It's Time to Move Forward.

Again, don't just rush things back to where they were before. The most important thing to realize after an eruption from the other side is that *they don't trust you yet.* You've managed to bring them back to the table to try negotiating again, but they're going to need a lot more than a few minutes of active listening to believe that you suddenly want to give them value when you weren't giving them much before.

It doesn't mean you can go back to persuading them that your win-lose (in your favor) proposal is actually good or intimidating them into accepting your terms. That's likely what caused the eruption in the first place!

Now your job is to **create new scenarios that deliver value for *both* parties, not just your side.** In this scenario, trust is gained (or regained) by actions, not words. If you want them to believe you'll create value for them, prove it by actually creating some.

If the source of eruption is linked to promises you didn't deliver on, ask them what they need, but don't let your fears push you to make additional promises you can't keep.

Being mindful during an eruption requires you to take time and practice using the C4U™ model during preparation, when you need to plan on how to handle emotions. It's almost impossible to manage a volcanic eruption without being under the control of your ego, especially if you didn't prepare and experience your emotions and practice being mindful ahead of time.

When They Demand to See or Talk to Your Boss

This is the ultimate dismissal from the other side, as it basically means they don't want to deal with you at all anymore. They want to talk to someone who has more power than you, in the hope that *that* person can give them what they want (since clearly you can't or won't).

This scenario is a big problem for three reasons. First, going back to your boss to say that your counterpart doesn't want to talk to you anymore might be a loss of face or reputation for you. You've done your best, and your best wasn't enough.

Second, this demand from the other side is almost always an escalation (if not an eruption!). Usually it sounds like "either you get your boss in here or we walk away right now." As we saw in the section where we discussed the other party threatening to walk away, this tactic triggers your emotions as your ego perceives it as an attack.

But the third reason is the most important one, because its threat doesn't come from the other side or your own ego. It comes from your boss.

See, your boss may be many things, but above all they are *busy*. Your boss does not have time to go through the whole process of negotiation or to learn the C4U™ system. That's what he hired *you* to do.

So, when your boss comes into a negotiation and sees the other side upset and emotional, their first and only instinct will likely be to maintain the relationship and get things back on track as fast as possible. It usually means conceding on whatever the other side wants—even if those are things you weren't prepared to offer, can't provide, or were planning to exchange for something of value for your side. This concession will set a bad precedent for the next time this client negotiates with you: they don't actually have to work with you, they just have to get your boss in the room to get what they want. That destroys all your credibility with them in the future.

Let's pause for a moment (C1) and be curious (C2) about what is happening inside of you:

1. What emotions come up when the other side wants to talk to your boss?
2. Which part of this situation brings up the most emotion—facing the other side's demand, dealing with your own sense of failure, or bringing in your boss?
3. What potential outcome(s) feel the worst to you? Why?
4. When have you dealt with this kind of demand to talk to a higher authority in the past?
5. What happened? How did you feel about it?

There's probably a lot here for you. You might be afraid of losing face, being judged by your boss, feeling trapped with no options, or ashamed you couldn't handle the deal yourself. Connect with self-compassion (C3). You don't need you to be your own enemy. Whatever you feel, it doesn't define or control you.

Now, let's find some ways to think about this that are not ego-driven (C4):

1. What if this request has nothing to do with you, so you don't have to take it personally?
2. What if you can still be in control without upsetting the other side?
3. What if this is an opportunity to demonstrate your negotiation leadership to your boss?
4. What if your boss is actually an ally here, not an enemy?

There are three options to choose between in this scenario. Mindfulness will help you choose the right one.

Option 1: Call their bluff outright by refusing to bring in your boss. This is the riskiest strategy because it's the easiest for your ego to take over. If you're on fire to prove yourself or want to dominate the other side, this option will appeal to you…and it will probably also blow up in your face. Only choose this option if you are 100% sure there's no ego behind your decision (and maybe not even then).

Option 2: Call their bluff more mindfully, through curiosity and hypothetical scenarios. This is similar to the scenario in the mountain rumbling chapter when the other side threatened to walk away. You might ask:

> Help me to understand why you are requesting to see my boss. Why do you feel the need to threaten to walk away from the deal if you don't?
>
> Are you saying that if I don't bring my boss, you are going to walk away after all the work we did together to get to this point?
>
> Why do you feel my boss will be able to give you anything more than I've been able to?
>
> If my boss isn't available right now, are you saying the deal is off?

A second mindful way to call their bluff would be to present a hypothetical scenario. You might say something like, "Okay, I can try to get my boss on the phone right now, but they'll tell you the same thing I just did." (Always be clear that you might not be able to reach them—unless you and your boss have specifically prepared for this moment, there's a good chance they might just not be able to answer the phone!) The idea is to present a united front, with enough confidence that the other side won't actually think you are bluffing. This is what we saw Alexis do. It's also something I've gone through myself more than once—it can be a stressful experience even when your boss does support you!

The catch here is that this is only a mindful option of you and your boss are in full agreement about the terms of the negotiation. Otherwise, it's just a lie that your ego wants you to tell. If the other side does say to call your boss, and your boss isn't actually on the same page as you are, you'll be in big trouble. Your ego doesn't care about that, but you sure do!

Option 3: Buy time. Offer to bring your boss to the next meeting, as long as they bring their boss as well. As your boss is very busy, it will go a long way to help free up your boss's time if he knows that your counterpart's boss will be present.

This is a great way to keep control of the situation in the moment without having to actually bring your boss into the picture. This way you'll have time to confer with your boss before he actually addresses the other side's demand.

Often this technique will work in your favor, forcing the other side to either back down on the demand or agree to wait. Sometimes it can backfire and make the other side suddenly get more emotional, though, since you're not actually giving them what they want. Remember, their goal is to get you to give in now, not continue the negotiation later. If that happens, you can either stand your ground with the tactics and mindfulness we discussed earlier in this chapter, or go back to option 2 and try to get your boss on the phone now—but be clear that it might not work, since you don't know your boss's availability at that exact moment.

Remember that your boss's goal is to make the deal happen as easily as possible—even if that means giving in. So if you go with option 3, bring mindfulness to meet with your boss and help them understand where the value is in the negotiation. You might want to propose workable concessions that could work in return for what the other side is demanding. If your boss still says "We will give in to save the deal," make sure the language you use to concede the demand doesn't create a precedent for future negotiations.

As with the objection handling section, you've now gone through a rough meeting and come out the other side—only this time, it was worse. So, this is your biggest celebration (C5)! What you just went through required you to use the C4U™ process during the preparation and through every moment of the meeting, and you did it.

That right there was the toughest personal challenge in negotiation. Managing a volcanic eruption while remaining mindful is the ultimate test in mastering the C4U™ system. And not only have you survived this meeting, but you've set a precedent for yourself in the next one.

Next time you find yourself facing an eruption, you'll be able to remember that last time you didn't let your ego control you, and you were successful in handling that eruption—so you can do it again.

At this point, you'd probably love to think that the negotiation is all done, the deal is closed, and everyone's ready to go home and *really* celebrate.

Unfortunately, successfully managing an eruption from the other side isn't *quite* the same thing as closing the deal. You're *almost* there, but there are a few more steps to take until you reach the summit.

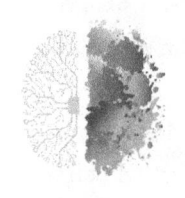

Chapter 11
MINDFULLY REACHING THE SUMMIT

"Everything you've ever wanted is on the other side of fear."
—George Addair

The Contract is Signed—Or is It?

One week later.

"Marco, it's good to see you again," said Jorge. "How long has it been?"

Marco still didn't look happy, but he shook hands with Jorge and Alexis as they entered the conference room. "About six years, I think," he said.

"Right, of course, the last time we renewed this contract."

Interesting, *Alexis thought.* No wonder Marco and Lucas were skeptical… they thought I was going to be another Jorge from the beginning. I'm really glad I've learned how not to be one!

Lucas came in last, closing the door behind him. "Are we all ready to sign? I've got the copies of the new contract right here."

"Yes, I think we're ready," said Jorge.

"Well, I'm almost ready," said Marco.

Alexis and Jorge traded confused looks. "Almost?"

"Yeah, I said almost," said Marco. "I was talking to our financial team yesterday, and it looks like we need a firm price on all reagent kits, both the

current and new generation, for the full length of the contract to make this work for us."

Jorge stiffened. "Excuse me? You brought us all together this morning to renew the contract, but now you need even more than we've already given you?"

Marco gave a smile that was almost a smirk. "I'm sorry to bring this up so late, of course, but I only just confirmed it yesterday myself."

Out of the corner of her eye, Alexis could see Jorge's right fist clench. Crap! He's getting ready to blow up at Marco. I'd better take this, and fast! *She put her hand on his arm.*

"Marco, I think what Jorge means to say is that we're surprised that such a significant need is coming up so late in the game. In fact, when Lucas and I discussed these particular points a few weeks ago, the conclusion we reached was your company still got what you needed with the contract as is."

Marco snorted. "Well, that was then, and this is now, clearly. So, if you'll agree, I'll sign right now."

Jorge sat forward as if to start speaking again, but Alexis squeezed his forearm again, giving him a smile, she hoped sent him a strong "I've got this" message. He held her gaze for a moment, then sat back again, apparently content to let her carry the ball.

"Okay, well, if that situation has changed, that's fine," said Alexis, "but we agreed to a deal we all felt was fair and equitable. We're not prepared to add value to your side of that deal without adding comparable value to our side. In order for us to agree with your latest request, we will need to remove similar value elsewhere in the contract. Or perhaps you were thinking of giving us something else in exchange for it?"

Marco groaned. "Come on, Alexis, this isn't that big a deal. We all want this contract renewed today; can't you just give in on this one thing?"

"No, Marco, I can't. Jorge and I came in here in good faith, to sign a contract we all agreed on last week. If you want to change that agreement, then the negotiation isn't over, and the contract isn't ready for renewal. If you want to take it back to the table and be part of the negotiations, we can do that—but I do need to remind you that there's only one more week before the current extension expires and all reagent kit prices revert to list price, not just the new-generation

ones. Is spending the next week trying to hammer out a new contract really what you want to do?"

"Okay, okay, okay, fine," said Marco, putting his hands up in front of him. "Lucas, what do you think?"

"Well, I agree that a firm price on both the current and new generation kits for the whole contract is more important than I initially thought it was, but I don't think it's worth killing the deal over. But what I think most of all is that we're going about asking for it the wrong way."

"Meaning?"

"Meaning that if we want something more from them, we should exchange it with something else we can offer them or ask them if there's anything more they'd like from us."

Alexis blinked. Wow, looks like Lucas HAS changed!

Marco rubbed his eyes wearily. "Alright, if you say so. Jorge, Alexis, is there anything you'd want to add to this deal to make firm pricing worth giving us for all five years?"

"I'll take this one," Jorge said, leaning forward.

Alexis was relieved that Jorge was stepping in, but also concerned—this wasn't a scenario they'd prepared for.

"Marco," Jorge started, "you are putting us in an uncomfortable position here with this late demand. I want you to know I don't like it. However, it feels like it's an important issue for you, so I'm prepared to work with you on it anyway."

Alexis was holding her breath.

"Now, I can't offer a firm price on the current kits, because we both know their volume will be reduced significantly throughout the contract timeframe. We have to have the increased price for those kits to maintain our margins, and besides, as their volume goes down, their pricing will have less impact on your overall budget. So, firm pricing on current kits isn't workable for us, but it won't really impact your bottom line anyway, which tells me Lucas and Alexis were right—you're getting what you want even with the price increase. Would you agree with that?"

Alexis couldn't believe what she was hearing. Jorge was actually giving Marco information instead of trying to get everything he could and potentially screw up the deal. Mentally she crossed her fingers.

"I guess so," said Marco. "Okay, fine, forget the current generation kits. What do you want in return for firm pricing on the new generation kits for the whole contract?"

Jorge thought for a moment. "If you agree to an additional contract year, to make it six years in total, and are willing to become a show site for our future customers, I can offer you firm pricing on those kits for all six years. What do you say?"

The room was silent for three long seconds. Jorge looked at Marco and didn't blink.

Marco threw up his hands. "Alright, alright, you win! I can work with those terms."

"Great!" said Alexis. "And really, we both win here, Marco. I know your goal is to get the most for yourself, but really look at these terms for a second. Can you imagine a deal that makes both of us so happy coming any other way?"

"Happy? Did I say I was happy?" Marco grumbled.

"No, but I know you well enough," put in Lucas. "You are happy with this contract—or at least you will be once it's signed, and we can start moving forward."

"I suppose that's true," said Marco, managing a small smile.

After a brief break to amend the contracts, all four signed the newly printed documents. Marco and Jorge left with quick handshakes all around, but Lucas lingered.

"Alexis, I was wondering…" he began.

"Yes?" she said.

"You mentioned that someone was mentoring you on how to negotiate the way you do. Could I…is there any chance I could meet them?"

Alexis grinned. "I think I could arrange that…as long as a twenty-two-year veteran thinks he could learn a new trick or two."

Lucas grinned back. "You know, I think he might just be able to do that."

"Great," said Alexis. "I'll set up a meeting."

○————————○

When You Face a Last-Minute Demand

What's the hardest part of the mountain to climb?

The last 100 feet before the summit.

That might seem entirely backward—it must be easier to climb the last 100 feet than the previous tens of thousands of feet, right? You're almost done!

Not so fast. The thing about the last 100 feet is that they're the *last* 100 feet. You're exhausted from hours or days of climbing. You're at a much higher altitude, which means your body is working much harder just to maintain baselines like heart rate and breathing. Speaking of breathing, there's a LOT less oxygen at the top of a mountain—you may even be breathing from a pressurized tank. Not to mention that the very top of the mountain is usually the steepest part. There's a good chance you'll be scaling a sheer cliff, not walking up a gentle slope.

The last 100 feet of the climb is the most challenging precisely *because* you're almost done. You want to relax and have a smooth, triumphant finish, but relaxing at that moment is more dangerous than any other moment of the climb. As counterintuitive as it might be, the last 100 feet are where you must pay the *most* attention and focus to the mountain, not the least.

This same principle holds true in negotiation.

After handling objections and managing eruptions, this is the stage where you will benefit the most from mindfulness. This is the moment where most negotiators leave money on the table because they are afraid to lose the deal.

How do you know you're in this stage of the negotiation?

Well, it might be obvious—if there's a contract on the table ready to be signed, it's pretty clear where you are.

But this stage actually starts sooner than that, and it can take some mindful attention to notice when you start transitioning into it.

There are four signs that indicate that you're close to reaching a final agreement:

1. Proposals and counterproposals are coming faster and closer together, and terms are changing less and less with each one.
2. Questions are getting more specific.
3. Objections are getting fewer and less strident.
4. Visible interest and excitement might be growing on both sides.

As these signs start to show up, you can be sure that a final agreement is coming up soon.

But don't let that lull you into a false sense of security!

When you are finally almost at the finish line, your adrenaline is flowing, and you are ready to celebrate—so ready, in fact, that you might be tempted to skip the last few minutes of your negotiation. That desire to skip forward is your ego talking, telling you that you've already reached the summit, and the last segment is super easy, so why stay focused or be mindful?

But just as you're starting to relax…the other side makes one more demand! The deal comes to a screeching halt as you have to decide what to do.

You might be wondering if this really happens. It can't be that common, can it?

Sorry to disappoint, but it happens *constantly*. In fact, it's far more common to have a negotiation where this *does* happen than one where it *doesn't*.

Many negotiators, especially people in charge of the buying process, are *trained to wait until the last minute to come up with an additional demand*. They know you're excited to get the deal done, and they know their request will trigger all kinds of fear in you about the deal falling through, losing all the hard work you've put in, and losing face with your boss. They know you'll want to say yes, just to make sure the deal is closed. And so they'll hit you with an extra demand in the hope that you'll be too excited or too scared to deny it to them.

And your ego falls right into their trap, going from carefree and calm to fight or flight faster than you can say "wait, what?" Typically, it will now want you to lash out at the other side for ruining your sense of being done.

"Seriously? We've just spent all this time hammering things out, and now you're asking for something else?"

"You are already getting a better deal than I wanted to give you. Quit pushing your luck."

"Come on, we're almost done…why are you dragging this out?"

"Look at everything I've already given you. Do you want my shirt as well?"

However true or accurate those sentiments may be, actually saying them to the other side is a great way to lose the deal!

Your ego might also want you just to give in so you can be done with this negotiation. If you are 300 feet from the summit of a mountain, and the Sherpa stops and says he won't take another step unless you pay him an extra $500, you might just hand over the money to get to the top. It's blatant extortion, but you're so close you can convince yourself you don't care.

And at the moment of reaching the top, you'll probably still be pretty happy. But as you start walking back down, you'll start to feel resentful that the Sherpa used being close to the top as a crowbar to get more money out of you than you originally agreed on.

This is why you don't want to let your ego convince you to give in just to be done already. If you give in to that last-minute demand, you will leave the meeting judging yourself for giving in under pressure.

So, let's stop for a moment here (C1). Notice how your blood pressure is increasing, your muscles are tensing, and your fear and frustration are rising. Then be curious around what's making your body respond that way (C2). Be an observer of your own emotions:

1. What emotions that are you experiencing?
2. Do you find yourself wanting to give in, or to push back? Why?
3. How does this last-minute demand impact your trust towards the other side? How excited would you be about negotiating with them again in the future?
4. When else in your life have you encountered last-minute demands like this? What happened? How did you feel about it? What emotions from those experiences are showing up here?

Take a few moments to breathe deeply. Bring compassion to this moment by remembering how your ego works (C3). Remember that these feelings aren't you, they're your ego reacting to feeling threatened. It's okay to recognize and feel them, but feeling them doesn't mean you have to let them control you.

Compassion, at this point, also looks like reminding yourself how far you've come and how *ready* you are to address this issue (C3). You've already been through weeks or months of negotiations. You've sought information, made proposals and counterproposals, handled objections, and managed erupting volcanoes. Even if you're new to negotiation or mindfulness, *you know what you're doing now.* You've got this! So, take one more deep breath and explore your choices (C4).

1. What if you can stay present and control your emotions?
2. What if the other side is using this as a tactic to see how much more they can get from you?
3. What if you can turn the tables and close the deal without damaging the relationship?
4. What can you offer to balance their new demand with new value?
5. What if you could stand your ground without antagonizing the other side?

As you explore alternatives, it will help to know there are two solid ways to answer a last-minute demand without giving in and losing your power. Which one you use depends on what they're asking for.

They may be asking for something small that you have no problem giving them. Maybe they want an introduction to your VP of a different division, or they want a testimonial from you about your work together. These small items are typically called "deal sweeteners," as they make the deal sweeter for one side without needing a lot of work from the other. You may have a list of deal sweeteners you're prepared to ask for in return; if so, propose a 1:1 exchange. Otherwise, you may simply want to accept their demand since it's such a small thing, and use that acceptance to create more goodwill down the line.

On the other hand, they may be demanding something significant that will change the overall value of the deal for you. In that case, don't let your ego take over—it will want you to push back or persuade.

Instead, mindfully let them know that you consider their last-minute demand a significant one and that you are surprised that they didn't bring it earlier in the conversation. By naming what's happening, you show them that you see what they're doing and aren't intimidated by it.

Then, as Alexis did with Marco, let them know that if that last-minute demand is important for them, you are prepared to agree—as long as there is an adjustment of equal value for you in the deal. Now they own their decision. You've given them a choice, and you are in control of the conversation. In my experience, more often than not the other party will say "No, that's okay," and forget the extra demand rather than give you anything else.

When They Ask If This is Your Final Offer

Sometimes this last-minute demand doesn't sound like asking for a specific thing. Instead, it sounds like, "Is that your best and final offer?" We saw this in the "volcanic eruption" part of Alexis's story, but it could just as easily show up here.

This is a tricky question because it pre-frames you to say, "Well, no, we could also add in these other benefits," to encourage the other side to agree to the deal. Even worse, it puts you in a position of having to guess what they want—if you say yes and they walk away, you'll know too late that the proposal wasn't right. But if you say no, they'll ask you for a better proposal that you may not be prepared to give them.

As always, your ego is going to want to take over here. Instead, take yourself through C4U™ to see what comes up for you in response to this question, what compassion you need to bring to the moment, and what some different choices might be.

One mindful response I've found success with is:

"Based on the priorities, concerns, and pain points you have shared with me, yes—this is my best and final offer. However, if you are willing to add new elements to the negotiation to give us both more value, I'm prepared to be flexible."

This is a very assertive and mindful way to let them know that the only way to change or improve on the current offer is to make sure both sides get more value, not just their side.

When Their Boss Makes the Last-Minute Demand

Remember my China story back in chapter 1?

I felt like things were going pretty well until 15 minutes before the meeting ended, when a senior executive from the other side came into the room, told me very aggressively that they needed net-180 payment terms or they'd walk away, and then glared at me until I gave in.

This tactic has one and only one goal: to intimidate you into giving up more value. Their boss doesn't care about damaging the relationship, they don't know all the details of the negotiation as they weren't present for them, and they know they have more power than you.

This is a negotiator's worst nightmare.

Not only does it introduce a last-minute demand, but it creates an entirely new situation where all the work, preparation, and information gathering you've done over the previous weeks is suddenly useless. This is like a freak snowstorm hitting right as you're approaching the mountaintop—you can't see anything, the path is gone, and the wind is strong enough to blow you right off the mountain! You may experience all kinds of emotions like fear, powerlessness, distrust, and anger.

A courageous, mindful approach when this happens is to call out the behavior and name what is happening: You might say something like:

"I'm surprised that you are coming in so late to the negotiation, as your colleagues and I have already agreed on a deal. I've already offered many concessions to your colleagues, and we've worked out an agreement that seemed workable to everyone until you came in just now. If you wanted to be part of the negotiation earlier, I would have been happy to include you then. If you'd like to reopen the negotiation, I'd be willing to schedule another meeting where you'd be part of the conversation. But making last-minute changes to a deal we've already agreed on isn't going to work for my organization unless we are removing something in the agreement of equal value."

This call-out turns the tables on them, letting them know you aren't going to be intimidated and puts the pressure on them to decide the next move. It also saves you from giving up power and putting yourself in a vulnerable situation.

If they push back and insist you give in to their demand right then and there (which they very likely will), take a quick timeout from the meeting to call your boss. This neutralizes the higher authority move that the other side has made. Your boss may back you entirely or tell you to meet the new demand in return for something else—either way, his authority will match the other side's.

Even if your boss tells you just to give in, you will create a much better precedent for future negotiations than if you gave in yourself. With your boss's authority behind the decision, it's easier to say that this is an exception for this specific situation, and that it won't apply and shouldn't be expected next time.

When *You* Make the Last-Minute Demand

Well...I'm going to go out on a limb here and say that if you're doing this, there's an excellent chance you're in your ego. If the demand is a deal sweetener, or if you really weren't clear about something significant you needed earlier on, okay, that's fine. Take the time to explain to your counterpart that you realized that you weren't clear enough, then bring them back to the drawing board with you and start again.

But if you find yourself wanting or needing to ask for something significant at the last minute, especially something that hasn't been part of the negotiation before now, you're most likely doing it because your ego told you to.

Consider:

Are you making a significant last-minute demand because you want to win?

Do you want to save face internally, within your organization?

Do you want to prove that you are a good negotiator?

Are you emotional (angry, furious, or upset) that you lost sight of your original objective and now you want to make the other side "pay" for the way they pushed you beyond your limit?

Does reading those questions upset you?

Do any of them upset you because they feel true for you?

Remember that the first step of the C4U™ system is being aware. Knowing that your ego reacts to these ideas will help you understand how it drives you to make a last-minute demand.

So, if you do find yourself in that situation, don't let that ego keep control! Take a moment to focus (C1) and be curious (C2) on why you really feel like you need to make this ask.

1. What are you afraid of?
2. What are you trying to prove?
3. How is your emotion playing out in the negotiation?
4. What don't you want to admit to yourself right now?

Since your ego is totally opposed to being curious about itself, make sure to connect with compassion for yourself (C3) even if you don't think you need it. Accept the situation for what it is. You have a deal ready to be closed, and it's probably a good one. Maybe it isn't perfect, perhaps you had to give more than you wanted or be extra creative to find solutions that worked for everyone, and perhaps you'll want to work toward a better deal in the future. But for right now, you have a deal you can live with. The emotion that's coming up around it may be valid, but it doesn't have to control you.

Let's explore what else could you do (C4):

1. What if, by making a last-minute demand, you are destroying trust and potentially damaging the relationship?
2. What if you could demonstrate your negotiation skills to your boss and your company without making a last-minute demand?
3. What if your demand will push the other side to take value away from the deal elsewhere?
4. What if the deal's faults and shortcomings aren't personal to you, they're just part of the best deal for both sides?

When you build a long-term working relationship with your counterpart, your objective is not to get the best deal all the time. Your objective should be to get the best deal on average. If this time, the agreement is a little more in their favor, next time, it will be a little more in yours. Just because the deal isn't perfect doesn't mean that you're an idiot or a failure. You can let this demand go.

On a final note, if you genuinely feel that this deal isn't worth taking, walk away and explain why. Don't let your fear or desire to prove yourself take control.

When You Are Considering Accepting a Bad Deal

Unfortunately, sometimes you really do need the deal more than you need to reject a last-minute demand. If they don't want to back down and you can't afford to walk away, you may decide to accommodate their demand because in the short term, getting something out of the negotiation is better than getting nothing. This often only happens when there's no other option—which means that if you're considering it, your job is to make 100% sure there is no other option.

Why? Because accepting a bad deal (or even a slightly less good deal) because of a last-minute demand sets a terrible precedent. Next time, the other side will almost certainly use the tactic again, expecting you to give in to them even more near the end and using your fear of losing the deal to leverage even better terms for themselves. The whole thing becomes a downward spiral for you and your company.

This is a big reason why preparation for each step of the negotiation is so necessary. By preparing in detail ahead of time, you'll know when it is the right time to accept a slightly worse offer, and when it's time to not accept an offer at all because the way things are now will be better in the long term.

Or to revisit the mountain analogy, every experienced climber knows when to turn back and say, "Not today, trying for the summit is too dangerous right now."

Let's tune out the external world (C1) and be curious around where those feelings are coming from (C2).

1. Why are you prepared to accept any deal?
2. What are you afraid of?
3. What are you trying to protect by accepting a bad deal?
4. Where do you position yourself between taking responsibility for what is happening vs. blaming the other side or your organization? Why is that?

Whatever is coming up, it's okay. Bring compassion (C3). You are where you are. There is no point in judging yourself, or letting your inner critic take over.

Let's explore how you could behave differently if you were not dictated by your ego (C4).

What if you can actually gain *more* respect from your counterpart by trading something valuable in exchange for their demand rather than just giving in to it?

What if you can gain *more* credibility by establishing firm boundaries and not letting the other side push you past your limit without damaging the relationship?

What if you could buy time by telling them that the way the deal has been laid out doesn't work for your organization, but you can create a counteroffer that meets their demand if they're willing to wait?

It's okay to back off from a deal, even if you think it's too late. If the deal truly falls beyond your limit, there is power in being able to tell the other side that you can't sign it and still be true to your company. If walking away now is the right move for your company, you can use mindfulness to help you make that move calmly and confidently—and come back to the table next time with more power.

You Have Reached the Summit! You Closed the Deal!

CONGRATULATIONS!!!!

This is your biggest accomplishment, the ultimate achievement in mountain climbing *and* in negotiation. It's the culmination of all the work you've put in over the last weeks or months, both in performing negotiation best practices and in learning and applying mindfulness.

It's time to mindfully celebrate (C5) in a big way!

You should be proud of yourself for freeing yourself from your ego. You just went through an ego-driven business process, and you were able to keep your ego at bay and be mindful while delivering value for both parties. Great job!

The first thing to do to celebrate is to recap what happened, and the moments where you behaved in ways you didn't think you could. Write down every moment where you were mindful and conquered an ego-driven reaction, every time you made a different choice than your ego wanted you to, every situation where you made a counterproposal based on seeking new information, handled an objection, managed an eruption, or dealt with a last-minute demand.

As you make that list, consider how different you are now than when you started. You're a very different—and much better—negotiator now than you were at the beginning of this process. Take a moment (C1) to feel it. Be curious (C2) about what it means for you to feel those differences in yourself. If these feelings include shame or frustration over mistakes you made, bring compassion (C3) and remember you did your best and achieved something great despite struggles along the way. And if you need to do anything else different going forward (including continuing to use this system in the future!), make that call right now (C4).

If you want to, share your list or other aspects of your experience with your family and friends. If you have a journal, spend some time writing about the process and what you learned. If you have a chance, use what you've learned to help others who need to learn how to negotiate more successfully.

Whatever you do, know that mindfulness will be part of your life and your negotiations for as long as you keep practicing it. And that will help you and everyone you negotiate with get what they want for years to come.

Celebration Time!

"Here you go, chips with extra guacamole," said the waiter. Mia stifled a laugh.

"Looks like Kamal wasn't kidding about your addiction," she teased as Alexis practically dove for the bowl.

"Hey, there's nothing wrong with needing my daily avocado fix," grumbled Alexis around a mouthful of chips.

"There certainly are worse addictions," joked Mia, snagging a chip of her own.

"Speaking of Kamal, I thought he and Jonathan and the rest were going to be here?" asked Alexis.

"They will be soon," said Mia. "But I wanted a few minutes just the two of us first. Tell me, what have you learned about mindfulness over these last few weeks?"

"Oh, man, so much! I'm not even sure where to start," said Alexis.

"Okay, let's start with C1. What have you learned about being mindful?"

Alexis thought for a moment. "I think I've learned that I CAN be mindful of what's coming up in tough moments. Before, I wasn't really aware of what my body was doing when I was afraid or angry, it all came over me so fast. Now I can slow down enough to pay attention to it."

"Good! How about C2?"

"I've definitely learned to be curious about what my ego sounds like!" said Alexis. "I've gotten a lot better at recognizing it in the moment. It still sneaks up on me more than I'd like, but once I do recognize it, I can usually tell what it wants me to do and why."

"C3?"

"You know, I thought I'd learned everything I needed about this when I faced what happened with my dad when I was eight," Alexis mused, "but then two really interesting things happened when I was negotiation with Lucas."

"Oh?" asked Mia. "What were those?"

"Well first, while Lucas and I were going back and forth on the proposal, I found myself revisiting that moment from my past from different angles. Sometimes it was about how I really was being a know-it-all, even though I didn't mean any harm by it. Sometimes it was about my dad really wanting to love me and not knowing how or feeling he could. Sometimes it was even about the schedule, how confusing and multi-layered it was."

"*That is interesting,*" *said Mia.* "*What did it teach you?*"

"*That's the second interesting thing,*" *said Alexis.* "*I started to feel compassion not just for myself, but for Lucas. And for the contract itself. And even for Jorge and Marco! It was really weird at first, but now that I'm past everything…I don't think I could have closed the deal without it. I'd have annoyed Lucas or triggered Jorge or mishandled Marco somewhere along the line—at least more than already I did!*"

Mia nodded thoughtfully. "*That's a really deep lesson, and one many people take a long time to learn. When you bring compassion to your own ego, you start to feel it for the ego of whoever you're talking to—even if it doesn't happen consciously. I'm really happy to hear you've discovered how valuable that is.*"

Alexis crunched more chips and guac. "*Me too!*"

"*Now, what about C4?*"

"*This was the most empowering part for me. Just exploring the idea that I COULD do something other than freeze up was like opening the door to a different world. It wasn't easy to step through that door at first, but the more I did, the more natural it got.*"

"*That's so good, Alexis. I'm really proud of you—you worked really hard on this over a fairly short timeframe, and it's really paid off. Now, I have to be the drill sergeant for just a second—don't stop here! C4U™ is in your toolbox now, but don't leave it there to rust.*"

"*I won't!*" *said Alexis.* "*I understand it now, and I used it well enough with this contract, but I know I have a lot more to learn.*"

"*I'm glad to hear that,*" *said Mia.* "*And you can always reach out to me if you need help with it again.*"

"*I will, for sure. But hey—you forgot to ask me what I learned about C5!*"

"*Oh really? And what DID you learn about it?*"

Alexis waved towards the door, where Jonathan was leading the "*C4U™ group*" *into the restaurant.* "*That celebrating is always better with friends!*"

You think you are a better negotiator?

Great!

How about being mindful in the rest of your life?

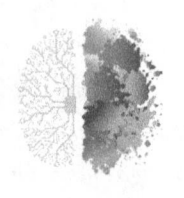

Chapter 12 / Bonus Chapter
EVERYDAY MOUNTAIN CLIMBING: HOW TO NEGOTIATE MINDFULLY IN YOUR DAILY LIFE

"The point of power is always in the present moment."
—Louise Hay

The main goal of this book is to help you learn the methodology and mindful practices of successful negotiation by taking you through a full negotiation process one step at a time.

But not all negotiations happen in official negotiation meetings! In fact, if you look closely at your day-to-day life, you'll likely notice negotiations happening all the time—with your boss and co-workers, with your spouse and kids, and with yourself.

Many of these negotiations take only a few moments. Some may take an hour or two. A few may even span days. But none of them last as long or involve as many different meetings or procedural steps as the official business negotiations we've been talking about up until now. And happily, most of them don't involve large emotional stakes—it's rare that a brief negotiation about who drives the team to lunch or whether you or your spouse makes dinner tonight has the potential to get you fired or torpedo your marriage.

That's the good news. The bad news is that nearly all of these daily negotiations happen without a lot of warning or advance notice. So, unlike official negotiations, you can't really prepare for them ahead of time. While each individual negotiation has a relatively small emotional charge or stake, dealing with a lot of them over time can start to raise those stakes, until eventually small negotiations like who drives or who makes dinner can make you feel like your job or your relationship are on the line.

So, what's the solution? How do you prepare to mindfully handle dozens or hundreds of small, low-stakes, day-to-day negotiations in your life without going through the whole multi-step methodology of successful negotiation practices?

The answer, as you may have guessed, is the C4U™ system.

Remember, this system is meant to be an ongoing practice, not just something you drag out from a dusty closet whenever you have a big negotiation coming up. The small things you encounter day-to-day don't typically have large emotional stakes. But they do still trigger *some* emotion from your ego, making a perfect ongoing training ground for the C4U™ system. Using the C4U™ system with these smaller negotiations will be easier than using it in bigger, more official ones—which helps you get used to using it.

Here's an example from my own experience:

I started writing this book almost three years ago. But as time passed, I found myself making all kinds of excuses to *not* write it:

- I'm flying home from a negotiation training, and I'm tired.
- I have only 15 minutes to write; I won't be able to accomplish anything.
- I don't feel creative today; tomorrow will be a better day for creativity.
- I want to read a novel or watch a movie instead.

After almost two years of this, people started asking me if I was still working on the book, or if it was ever going to come out. I'd tell them, "It's coming along, but it's a big job" or "I've written about half of it so far" (even though that wasn't entirely true). I'd tell myself to get back to work, have a few days of productive writing, and then start making excuses again.

This situation, I realized, was a textbook example of negotiating with myself—and I was losing. I wanted to write this book, but when I thought about writing it in the context of my daily life, I kept finding excuses not to do it.

So, I decided to take my own advice and use the C4U™ system to approach the situation mindfully. I turned off my phone, closed my laptop, and sat quietly for a few moments to focus on what was coming up in my body when I thought about writing the book (C1).

I found that I was carrying a lot of tension and pressure around the idea of the book. When I thought about it, my shoulders would tighten, my face would tense up, and my breath would get shorter and shallower—not to the point of panic, but definitely to the point of wanting to think about something else.

I asked myself why I was feeling so much pressure and tension around writing this book (C2).

The first few answers I came up with were all about fear of things I felt I couldn't control:

- I'm afraid of being seen as a fraud.
- I'm afraid no one will care about my book.
- I'm afraid of failing—whether that means not finishing the book at all or writing a book that doesn't grow my business or change readers' lives.

Those all made sense, because my ego clearly was responding to those fears by finding excuses for me to not write the book so it could feel protected from those fears. But I felt like there was something more to understand, something deeper. So, I kept asking myself why, and eventually, I came up with this:

I'm overwhelmed by the writing process. I have so much to say, but I don't have a clear structure for saying it, so sitting down to write feels futile. I don't know if I can actually do this, so trying feels like setting myself up for failure. I think I need help.

I felt embarrassed, deficient, and ashamed of myself for not being a better writer, more capable, more on top of things. After all, I'd been teaching and training with this material for years—why couldn't I just sit down and write about it? I was even afraid to tell my wife what I'd come up with, thinking she'd judge me for it.

I knew I had to find some compassion for myself (C3). I started by calling out my ego more directly, letting it know that I knew the thoughts of shame and embarrassment were its triggers, not from my real, authentic self. I allowed the little voice telling me I wasn't good enough to float past me, and I listened for what my mind and soul wanted to tell me. Here's what I heard: *It's okay to ask for help. Getting help in a difficult area makes you stronger, not weaker.*

That thought allowed me to start asking different questions and making different choices than my ego wanted me to! Where my ego wanted me to either push through the book or quit, I started to consider what might be good third or fourth options (C4).

And what came to me almost immediately was this: *You've had a business coach in the past who helped you get past some big blocks in your work—why not find a book coach to help you do the same thing with this book?*

Long story short, that's exactly what I did. I hired a book coach to help me with the structure and clarity of the text, hold me accountable to a regular writing practice to get the book done, and work with me to make sure the final product was the best quality it could be. And you're holding the results of that decision in your hands right now—a finished, published book that I felt empowered to write without excuses or overwhelm.

To be fair, this example was a bit bigger and higher-stakes than many you'll encounter in your day-to-day life. But it's still a great depiction of using the C4U™ system in a negotiation with yourself!

In the rest of this chapter, I'll share some common personal and professional scenarios where you can use the C4U™ system in your daily life.

PERSONAL
Deciding whether to go to the gym before work

We negotiate with ourselves dozens of times a day, often around whether to do something we don't really want to do right now but know will be good for us—like going to the gym. Usually, we make these decisions from our egos, which push us to do something more pleasurable instead (like hitting a drive-thru on the way to work instead of getting in a workout) or put it off for later (like saying you'll go to the gym after work, even though you know you probably won't).

Mindfully negotiating with yourself looks like this:

C1: Take a moment to pause from the decision process. Allow yourself to let go of the need to decide something right now, and instead focus on the moment.

C2: Be curious about why you really don't want to go to the gym. Maybe you don't feel attractive compared to the people you see there, or you feel overwhelmed because you have way too many things on your plate, or you're tired because you stayed up too late the night before watching Netflix.

C3: Bring compassion to yourself. Remember that you're going to the gym for yourself, not for anyone else, and that everyone had to start somewhere. Or consider that you don't have to do everything all at once, and that you have more time than you think. Or remind yourself that everyone has off days and that staying up too late last night doesn't make you a failure today.

C4: Make a choice to do something other than what your ego wants. Maybe that means you go to the gym after all, but it could also mean that you go for a walk over your lunch break instead, or do some push-ups and lunges right now so you can do *some* exercise before tackling your busy day, or even skip the gym today to catch up on sleep…If you are watching Netflix two or three evenings in a row, set an alarm to signal bedtime

This process doesn't always look like a negotiation because it's happening inside your head, but it still qualifies. Ultimately, you're making a decision between two or more conflicting desires you have, including your ego, and the C4U™ system can help you find a workable path forward that feels good and gets you what you really want.

Arguing With Your Spouse or Partner

Anytime we argue with a loved one, emotions get triggered. We feel judged, unseen, unheard, disrespected, and even unloved—even though beneath our ego's screams, we know the other person loves us and we love them!

Let's say you just got home from work, and your spouse starts yelling at you because it was your turn to pick up the kids from daycare…and you forgot. They got a call from the daycare asking where you are and saying that you'll be charged a penalty for picking them up late, and then had to leave work early and sit through an extra-long commute to get the kids. Your spouse is not happy, and you can already feel yourself going into fight-or-flight mode.

C1: Stop, take a deep breath, and focus on what's happening inside of you. Specifically, you really don't like being yelled at. Yes, you made a mistake, but yelling at you about it feels like your spouse is overreacting and taking her frustration out on you—which you don't need after the frustrating day at work you had, which is what made you forget about picking up the kids in the first place.

C2: Why does being yelled at bother you so much? Maybe because it reminds you of your mom yelling at you as a kid, which always made you feel incompetent. Or maybe because your boss yells at you all the time and having your spouse do it feels like adding insult to injury.

C3: Bringing compassion to this moment first looks like reminding yourself that you didn't do this on purpose and that making a mistake doesn't make you a bad person or a bad spouse, any more than making a mistake as a kid made you incompetent. Nobody's perfect, and no one has to be—including you. But compassion also looks like realizing that this moment isn't about you, it's about your spouse. Your mistake made their day a lot worse, and that needs to be acknowledged here. Compassion is about being gentle with yourself, but it's not about making excuses.

C4: First, make a choice *not* to do what your ego wants you to do—whether that's yelling back, running away, or anything else drastic or dramatic. Remember the erupting volcano! Erupting in response never helps. If you need to take some time to cool off and process things, that's fine. Next, be willing to give your spouse what they need—which is most likely a sincere, excuse-free apology that lets them know you're aware you messed up and regret how it made their life harder. Finally, think about what you can do going forward to avoid having this particular scenario repeat itself. Maybe that means hiring a sitter to pick up the kids or going into work a bit earlier so you'll be freer to pick them up or finding a different daycare that can keep the kids later without a penalty.

Expressing Your Needs with Assertiveness and Empathy

It can be really hard to tell another person that you need something—especially if that need puts additional pressure on them. But just ignoring the need isn't healthy for you!

Let's say you need time for yourself this weekend, and you'd like your spouse to take full responsibility of the kids so you can take a much-needed break. Your ego would tell you to express this need in one of two ways: either aggressively (where you dominate your spouse into doing what you want) or fearfully (where you half-heartedly ask for what you want, ready to give in if your spouse gets upset).

The first option doesn't work because it will trigger your spouse's anger. The second doesn't work because it doesn't honor your needs. Is there a third option, something that honors what you need while still respecting your spouse?

Let's find out:

C1: Sit with your need for personal space and time this weekend. Let your body tell you how strongly you need it. Let your mind show you how valuable that time is.

C2: Be curious as to why you're afraid to ask for this time. Is it because you're afraid of your spouse being angry? Are you ashamed at having to ask for a break when your spouse works just as hard as you AND does more to take care of the kids and the house? Are you afraid of being selfish (or at least perceived to be selfish)? Is it difficult for you to express what you need because your parents never let you express your needs (or never valued them when you did)?

C3: Have compassion for where you're coming from. There's nothing wrong with having difficulty expressing your needs, and there's nothing wrong with *having* needs in the first place. Taking care of yourself doesn't make you selfish, as long as you do it in a way that allows your spouse to feel that you still care about them as well.

C4: What if you could express your needs assertively and still show respect and care for your spouse? Or what if you didn't have to worry about their reaction because you trusted yourself to express your needs respectfully? What might that look like? From here, you can find ways to balance your need for some personal time with respect for your spouse's needs and practice expressing that need assertively and clearly.

Holding a Grudge

A grudge is what happens when the ego feels threatened or judged...and then holds onto that feeling for weeks, months, or even years, so that whenever you think about the object of your grudge, your thoughts are always angry, defensive, and hurt. No fun, right?

Let's say that several years ago, your older sister told you that you never invite the family to your place for holidays, that she always has to host the holiday gatherings, and that you're only looking to go to someone else's house to celebrate—basically, she called you a mooch and a freeloader and implied that you weren't a fully contributing member of the family.

What she said hurt a lot, and your ego decided that if she's going to insult you like that, you don't need to talk to her ever again. Fast forward a while, and you haven't seen your family for holidays in years, and anytime one of them brings up your sister, you snap at them and change the subject.

Now imagine receiving the same comment from your sister and having the C4U™ system on your side.

C1: Breathe deeply and allow your body to feel the pain and tension her statement brings up.

C2: Ask yourself why this comment hurts so much. Maybe because it takes your situation out of context—you don't invite the family over because you live in a small apartment with no room to entertain, you work two low-paying jobs that don't leave you much extra money or time, and most family members live closer to her anyway. Maybe because she has a big house and lots of money, and it feels like she's judging you for not having those things yourself (and maybe you're judging yourself a bit for not having them). Maybe because you and she have always been close confidantes, so this statement felt like a betrayal.

C3: Acknowledge where you are without self-judgment. Your lifestyle is what it is—whether you're happy with it or working to make it better. You know you would host holiday gatherings if you felt able to do so, and that you aren't trying to mooch off your sister. Finding compassion for yourself will help you show compassion for your sister—maybe she's feeling like she has to carry the whole burden herself, or maybe her budget is stretched thinner than it looks.

C4: The main choice here is to stop your ego from letting you turn the pain of this statement into a grudge in the first place—or to dissolve the grudge if you've been holding onto it for a while already. Maybe you can share with your sister (and the rest of the family) how you'd like to host gatherings but don't feel able to right now. Maybe you can suggest a potluck celebration or a gathering at a favorite restaurant, so your sister doesn't feel like she has to do everything.

Do you feel the difference in energy here by being mindful? It's not about putting yourself down or making yourself wrong so the other person can be right—that's what usually leads to holding a grudge to begin with. Instead, it's about putting your ego aside and sensing what other options might be on the table that makes everyone feel heard and respected.

People-Pleasing

Sometimes we feel like we have to do what makes someone else happy, even if it doesn't actually make *us* happy, because our ego is afraid of upsetting them or losing their favor. For example, let's say your mom wants you to call her twice a week. You have a busy life and don't feel you need to call her that often. But you know when you don't call her twice a week, she gets upset and texts and calls you every day until you call her back, so you make yourself call her twice a week just to avoid upsetting her. The calls are short, awkward, and unhappy, but at least they happen.

Don't get me wrong here. I'm not telling you never to call your mom, and I'm not saying every mom gets upset unless they get twice weekly calls. What I am saying is that doing something to avoid upsetting someone else is like giving into an unworkable demand in a negotiation just to keep the other side at the table. It may feel like you're picking the lesser of two evils, but really, you're setting a precedent of hurting yourself to make another person feel good—which will always become a downward spiral in the long term.

So, when your mom sends you another "when are you going to call me back?" text, try bringing mindfulness to the situation.

C1: Pause, breathe, and whatever you do, *don't* immediately reply. Take a moment to connect with yourself first.

C2: Ask yourself why you feel so conflicted about calling your mom twice a week. Is it because the conversations are always about her and never about you? Do you feel like she's trying to control you? Are you afraid that if you don't call her twice a week, she will resent you or stop loving you? Does her demand remind you of difficult moments growing up with her (i.e., did you feel she was demanding and controlling when you were a kid)?

C3: Compassion here looks like realizing that whatever you're feeling is valid and that being frustrated with your mom doesn't make you a bad son or daughter. It is also understanding it's okay to want to do things differently than someone else does, even when that person's opinion or favor means a lot to you. Taking care of yourself is just as important as pleasing someone else—often more so. Recognize that by doing what *you* need to do for yourself, you set yourself up to give others the love or service or attention they want from a place of genuine care rather than frustration.

C4: Your ego wants you to just call your mom back and put up with her demands so she doesn't get upset—or for you to get even more upset at her for making them in the first place. But you don't have to do either of those things! The courageous choice here might be to hold a firm boundary of calling her once a week and ignoring her texts and calls in between. It might be to start calls with her by sharing what's happening in your life, so they aren't all about her and never about you. It might even be to tell her that you love talking to her, but you don't want to feel obligated to do it, and so you need to find a call schedule that makes *both* of you happy.

People-pleasing usually happens because we hope the other person will change if we only give them what they want. Problem is, by giving them what they want, we tell them they don't have to change! The truth is that other people don't change until *you* do. And changing yourself means combating your ego, which means being mindful.

PROFESSIONAL
Keeping (and appearing) Busy at Work

In the Western world today, being busy is a badge of honor. The busier you are, the better. So, it's easy to fall into a cycle of busyness where every spare minute gets filled with work. Email, calls, meetings, project deliverables, reports...the more you get done, the more there is to do, and the busier you look, the better it looks to your boss and co-workers.

The problem is, just being busy for the sake of being busy is no guarantee of productivity. Switching between tasks or multitasking actually makes you *less* productive. So does working yourself into a stupor and never taking breaks to recharge. And looking busy all the time might look great to your boss...until you collapse at your desk from burnout.

Clearly, you need to accomplish your goals and meet your job requirements, and you want to do them well. But why do you need to be busy all the time—or be *seen* being busy all the time? Let's apply some mindfulness to this question.

C1: Stop. Really, whatever you're doing at work right now, hit the pause button. I promise, unless its deadline is literally an hour away, whatever it is will keep for five minutes. This won't be easy—your ego will scream at you to keep working! Let it scream and allow yourself to ignore the noise and listen to your body and mind. Are your shoulders in knots? Can you barely keep your eyes open? Do you feel like you need a sixth cup of coffee? Are you wondering how it's already 3:00 PM, and you managed to miss lunch...again?

C2: Be really curious about why you're making yourself so busy. Do you feel that you demonstrate your level of competency by being busy? Are you so busy because you can't manage your time and/or priorities well (and maybe don't want to admit it)? Are you afraid to delegate some tasks because you feel like *you* must do it all yourself? Are you trying to get appreciation or recognition from your boss or your peers?

C3: Keep breathing. Consider that a lot of people are in this exact same situation—you are not alone. Being too busy, or making yourself busy for unhelpful or unhealthy reasons, doesn't make you a bad person or a bad worker. You can still perform well and meet your goals without running yourself into the ground.

C4: Imagine you were helping someone else to be more efficient with their time. What would you recommend? This is a helpful exercise because we are nearly always our own biggest blind spots—looking at our own issues as if it's someone else's can help us see that issue more clearly. Maybe you need to learn how to say no (or at least "not yet/not now") when you have too much on your plate to take on something new. Maybe letting go of perfectionism and learning to trust your colleagues or team would help, so you could feel more comfortable delegating tasks to them. Maybe you need to realize that success and recognition come from achieving good results, not from appearing busy. And maybe it's time to give yourself a bit of tough love and recognize that you're not as efficient or effective or even competent as you might think you are—and ask for help to get better.

Whatever the answer looks like for you, mindfulness will help you find it without making the process feel like one more thing to do on your long list!

Getting Overwhelmed By Your Workload

This sounds similar to being busy, doesn't it? The difference is that usually when you're keeping busy or trying to appear busy, you're doing it to yourself—constantly adding new tasks, never taking breaks, etc. Dealing with an overwhelming workload is more often an external scenario—you have too much to do because your boss or your customer won't stop giving you work today before you've finished the work they gave you yesterday, last week, or last month. It feels like you are running on a treadmill with no end in sight.

C1: As with being busy, C1 means stopping what you're doing—no matter how urgent it seems to be. Without purposeful stillness, you'll never break the cycle of putting out the next fire, and the next, and the next, until you collapse at your desk.

C2: Why does your workload feel so out of control? Is it because you struggle to set and keep clear priorities within your workload—or even to understand what's most important? Do you say yes to everything assigned to you for fear of upsetting your boss? Are you afraid to ask for help? Do you find yourself constantly interrupted or distracted while you're trying to get work done?

C3: In an urgent, high-pressure job environment, it can be easy to feel shame for falling behind or not feeling like you're on top of your game. Don't fall for that! That's your ego trying to control you with emotion. Instead, you can remind yourself that there's nothing wrong with needing help sometimes, and/or that prioritizing and setting healthy boundaries will make you perform better, not worse.

C4: Your ego may want you to freak out, lash out, or just work harder—but those aren't your only options. Perhaps the courageous choice is to have a conversation with your boss about the priorities of your position, so you know what's most important and what can be held off until there's more time. Maybe when your boss asks you to do one more thing, you can tell them assertively that you don't have time to add that project to your current task list and ask them to help you prioritize that list. If interruptions or distractions are part of the problem, perhaps setting aside two hours a day where you close your door, turn off all notifications, and hold a firm "no interruptions" boundary so you can focus on deep work would be a good solution. If these solutions don't feel good, you can try conditional exploring with yourself to creatively find others.

No matter how overwhelming things may seem, you do have options. Mindfulness can help you find them.

Speaking Up in a Meeting

Meetings are confusing. If you speak too much, you can come off as self-important, but if you don't speak enough, you can come off as disconnected or not paying attention. Especially since speaking up can be terrifying! Let's say you just got promoted or moved into a new department, and you're in your first few meetings with a new group of people. You might be afraid to speak up at all since you're too junior and/or the "new guy." But you can't just stay silent forever, or your boss will start to wonder if the promotion or move was right for you after all. You're between a rock and a hard place. Fortunately, mindfulness can help.

C1: It might feel like you're already paused here if you're not saying anything, but go deeper. Don't just sit there without talking—you were already doing that! Take a moment to look inward and listen to your mind and body.

C2: Be curious about why you're afraid to speak. Do you feel incompetent or outclassed around senior executives, like it's not your place to speak in front of them? Are you afraid your ideas might be laughed at or dismissed because you're new/junior? Are you desperate to make a good impression and worried that anything you say might mess it up? Did something happen when you were younger that made you fear rejection from bosses or authority figures?

C3: Connect with compassion. Everyone has been the "new guy"! And everyone has had their ideas rejected at times. That's how they learn to come up with better ideas. Nothing about any of that is personal to you. You don't need to judge yourself or be ashamed or fearful because you're new or junior or still learning—in fact, being where you are now is a necessary step on the path to being where those executives are in the future. You can also remember that you were been invited to this meeting because your boss believes you can make a contribution. Hence, you belong here, and your voice has a right to be heard.

C4: Perhaps coming to each meeting with questions prepared ahead of time will help you feel more prepared to speak. Maybe you can write your idea down on a piece of paper when you propose it, so if it gets rejected, you can pin the rejection on the paper and take it less personally. Writing out some of the evidence in favor of your idea might also help you feel ready to share it, so that if someone is skeptical or asks questions, you'll be prepared to answer them. Feel free to get creative here—what are some ways you can make a contribution without giving in to fear?

Preparing For a Presentation

This is a tough scenario for *lots* of people—speaking in front of a group, presenting a project or idea and answering questions, navigating technology, possibly managing a team or group, and of course, fitting all of the prep work in on top of everything else you have to do. Lots of places for your ego to stage a hostile takeover…which usually looks like procrastinating on the presentation until the day before, and then frantically scrambling to throw something together at the last minute. Let's not let that happen this time.

C1: Hit the pause button on whatever work you're doing (or procrastinating on) for the presentation. Connect with yourself before your ego can seize control.

C2: What's really coming up around wanting to procrastinate on this presentation? Are you afraid it will fall apart? Are you terrified to speak in front of a group? Are you feeling overwhelmed?

C3: Bring compassion to help you stay in the moment without judging yourself. Thousands of people, likely including everyone you'll be presenting to, have had to do exactly what you're doing. And they all got through it! You will, too.

C4: If your ego wants you to procrastinate on getting the presentation ready (and then freak out at the last minute when you still have all the work to do), consider a few other options instead. Perhaps you could break the presentation down into smaller sections and do them one at a time. Maybe you need to get some help with the technical or design side, so you don't have to try to figure it all out yourself. Or you could ask your boss or another mentor in your company to help you make a plan for presenting successfully. You might even talk to a colleague who does a lot of presentations and ask for some tips on speaking to a group comfortably.

Receiving Feedback From Your boss

We've all heard something like "you're doing good work, but your attitude could use some work, so work on that, and you'll be fine" or "you're a solid worker, but you'll never be a leader, so just keep doing what you're doing" at some point—maybe even a few points. Receiving feedback from a superior can be a field day for your ego—anything less than 100% positive triggers the ego's survival instinct. In that moment, it's as easy as breathing to hyper-focus on the negative pieces and go into fight-or-flight.

Mindfully receiving feedback is difficult, but doable. Here's what it looks like:

C1: Take a deep breath and use your practice of finding stillness in a tough moment. Allow your ego's desire to react to flow past you as you look inward.

C2: Why are you hurt or upset by this feedback? Is it because you feel unfairly judged? Are you afraid that the feedback will mean losing out on something you really want (a raise, a promotion, your boss's favor)? Or are you ashamed because the feedback is right on and you don't want to admit it?

C3: Connect with compassion right away. Recognize that everyone struggles to receive constructive criticism—and frankly, a lot of people struggle with *giving* it well, too. Chances are your boss didn't mean to be harsh (possibly they were in their ego!) Also, remember that your ego always wants you to consider feedback as extreme—either you're doing great, or you're a total failure who's about to get fired, nothing in between. But the reality is that feedback is almost never that extreme. There are nearly always things you're doing well, just as there are nearly always things you could work on. That's called being human. Stay with this compassion as long as you need—even if that means taking a break before responding to the feedback.

C4: The key here is to avoid letting your emotions carry you away (which is what your ego wants you to do). You are not going to learn anything if you are emotional, upset, pissed-off, or ready to fight back—and learning from the feedback must be your goal. Otherwise, you'll just get the same feedback in a few months and have to deal with this exact situation again. So, instead of letting your emotions run wild, observe them, thank them for trying to protect you, and then dismiss them. Then ask yourself what you can learn from what you're hearing and be open to the answers that come—even if they are hard to hear. You may also want to ask your boss or another mentor for guidance on how to improve the areas they gave negative feedback on. You might even find a way to disagree with them without emotion and have a conversation about the difference between what your boss perceived about your work and what you actually did.

As you can see, there are many daily and regular occasions to use mindfulness to keep your emotions from ruining situations. You can apply mindfulness to smaller, lower-stakes scenarios in daily life and not just the big scary business negotiations this book was written to help you with. Doing so helps you when you *do* get into those negotiations, and you'll already be comfortable and ready to take on your ego.

After each C4U™ session, don't forget to celebrate (C5) what you have been through. Each time you are mindful, it is a moment where your ego has relinquished control over you, and you're free to be yourself. Celebrate those moments and how great they feel!

CONCLUSION

"Have the courage to follow your heart and intuition.
They somehow know what you truly want to become."
—Steve Jobs

You've just finished the journey of learning about mindful negotiation. Now what?

Pause for a moment.

What's coming up for you now? Are you confused, overwhelmed, scared, excited, inspired? What did you learn about yourself? Are you pumped up to embrace mindfulness, or afraid it might not work for you? What is your little voice telling you about everything you've just read?

What feels good and natural about what just came up? What feels like *you*, not just your ego? What's telling you that it's okay to think or feel a certain way, that everyone deals with those thoughts, that you're a human who's learning something new and not a robot who has to get everything right the first time? How can you let go of judgment and accept what is?

What choices can you make right now around mindfulness to move forward without your ego taking over? What courage will it take to make those choices? What will you need to do to find and use that courage?

What can you celebrate learning from this book? What will you take with you that will help you have more successful negotiations going forward?

Okay, clearly, you see what I did there. But I didn't do it just to shove the C4U™ system at you one more time.

I did it because it's easy to read a book and then forget about it, or think "that was cool, now on to the next thing." And a few weeks or months later, you're back in your comfort zone, with your ego fully in control…then the next big negotiation comes up, and you've forgotten everything.

This is exactly what your ego wants. Your ego doesn't want you to learn. It wants you to continue behaving as it is telling you to do. Your training knowledge is in your head, but you don't use it because it's easier (and less threatening to your ego) not to.

If you're serious about getting better at negotiation, simply reading this book won't be enough. Even using the C4U™ system a couple of times won't get you there. As Mia told Alexis, nobody became an elite athlete or world-class musician the first time they stepped on a court or picked up an instrument, and no great negotiator got that way without constant practice. That's why I included the chapter about smaller, everyday uses for the C4U™ system, and why I brought the system up yet again at the beginning of this conclusion.

Your assignment, should you choose to accept it, is to practice being mindful until it becomes automatic. The methodology for value-creating negotiation will always be here to reference, but mindfulness isn't something you can just keep on a shelf until you need it. Mindfulness, in general, and the C4U™ system specifically, is meant for everyday use. Practice them until they become second nature, and I promise you will see your negotiations improve dramatically.

To help with that, here are three final questions for you to consider:

1. Where in this book was mindfulness the most challenging for you?
2. Which stage(s) of negotiation was the scariest or most triggering for your ego?
3. Which teachings in this book resonated with you most deeply?

Being curious about these questions will help you find the areas where mindfulness will help you the most as both a person and a negotiator. You have grown tremendously since the beginning of this book, but the journey is only now beginning.

Keep mindfully growing, and soon enough, you will see a difference in the outcomes you can negotiate.

Sincerely,

Gaëtan Pellerin

ABOUT THE AUTHOR

Gaëtan Pellerin has spent the last ten years as a negotiation consultant-coach, helping negotiators get better with their skills, preparing and rehearsing for their upcoming live deals. He also has consulted many organizations on their strategies and established best practices for product launches, technology retirement, and the internal negotiation decision process.

Before beginning his consulting work, Gaëtan held several senior sales and marketing management roles that allowed him to negotiate multimillion contracts in Japan, China, Thailand, Europe, and North America.

Gaëtan is passionate about people. He has always been intrigued by what is behind the scene of each of us: motivation, fears, emotions, desires. His desire to be more involved with people's development led him to get his certification as an Integral Development Executive coach. He has focused on his personal growth for the last ten years.

Gaëtan's clients describe him as "an incredibly talented coach," "critical to our success," "well worth the investment—I haven't worked with anyone of Gaetan's caliber," and "an insightful, experienced negotiator, who brings his many years of global experience—along with his coaching expertise—to every engagement to deliver massive value."

He has a B. Sc degree from the University of Montreal and an M.B.A from the University of Sherbrooke. Gaëtan now lives in Scottsdale, AZ, and when he is not helping other people with a negotiation or personal growth, you will find him hiking by himself or with his wife Chris, riding his mountain bike, or cooking with a good glass of wine. He is fascinated with sharks (loves to dive in their environment) and is always looking for the next book that he can learn from.

REFERENCES

Chapter 1
1. Vlachakis and all, In Vivo. 2018 Jul-Aug (859-870)

Chapter 3
1. Teper et al. Social Cognitive and Affective Neuroscience, Volume 8, Issue 1, January 2013. Meditation, mindfulness and executive control: the importance of emotional acceptance and brain-based performance monitoring. Pages 85-92
2. Cardaciotto et al. Sage Journals, June 2008. The Assessment of Present-Moment Awareness and Acceptance: The Philadelphia Mindfulness Scale
3. Schmeichel et al. Journal of Personality and Social Psychology, Vol 85(1), Jul 2003. Intellectual performance and ego depletion: Role of the self in logical reasoning and other information processing. Pages 33-46
4. Caseda et al. Psy ArXiv preprints. Do mindfulness-based interventions enhance executive control? A systematic review and meta-analysis of randomized controlled trials in adults. March 2019